PRISM

READING AND WRITING
TEACHER'S MANUAL

4

Jessica Williams

with
Wendy Asplin
Christina Cavage
Alan S. Kennedy
Jeanne Lambert

CAMBRIDGE
UNIVERSITY PRESS

CAMBRIDGE
UNIVERSITY PRESS

University Printing House, Cambridge CB2 8BS, United Kingdom

One Liberty Plaza, 20th Floor, New York, NY 10006, USA

477 Williamstown Road, Port Melbourne, VIC 3207, Australia

4843/24 2nd Floor, Ansari Road, Daryaganj, Delhi – 110002, India

79 Anson Road, #06-04/06, Singapore 079906

Cambridge University Press is part of the University of Cambridge.

It furthers the University's mission by disseminating knowledge in the pursuit of education, learning and research at the highest international levels of excellence.

www.cambridge.org
Information on this title: www.cambridge.org/9781316625446

First published 2017

20 19 18 17 16 15 14 13 12 11 10 9 8 7 6 5 4 3 2 1

Printed in the United Kingdom by Latimer Trend

A catalogue record for this publication is available from the British Library

ISBN 978-1-316-62544-6 Teacher's Manual 4 Reading and Writing
ISBN 978-1-316-62474-6 Student's Book with Online Workbook 4 Reading and Writing

Cambridge University Press has no responsibility for the persistence or accuracy of URLs for external or third-party internet websites referred to in this publication, and does not guarantee that any content on such websites is, or will remain, accurate or appropriate. Information regarding prices, travel timetables, and other factual information given in this work is correct at the time of first printing but Cambridge University Press does not guarantee the accuracy of such information thereafter.

CONTENTS

SCOPE AND SEQUENCE

UNIT	WATCH AND LISTEN	READINGS	READING SKILLS	LANGUAGE DEVELOPMENT	
1 CONSERVATION *Academic Disciplines* Architecture / Information Technology / Urban Planning	Preserving CDs at the Library of Congress	1: Are We Living in the Digital Dark Ages? (article) 2: To the County Board regarding Cook County Hospital (letters)	*Key Skills* Identifying an argument Identifying supporting details *Additional Skills* Using your knowledge Previewing Understanding key vocabulary Reading for main ideas Reading for details Making inferences Skimming Identifying purpose Synthesizing	Time expressions Compound adjectives	
2 DESIGN *Academic Disciplines* Graphic Design / Marketing	The Role of Helvetica Font in Graphic Design	1: What Makes a Successful Logo? (textbook chapter) 2: Rebranding and Logos (textbook chapter)	*Key Skills* Taking notes in outline form Making inferences *Additional Skills* Previewing Understanding key vocabulary Reading for main ideas Reading for details Identifying purpose Predicting content using visuals Making inferences Synthesizing	Describing emotional responses Paraphrasing	
3 PRIVACY *Academic Disciplines* Business / Law Enforcement / Media	Computer Fraud: Celebrity Hacking	1: Cyber Harassment (article) 2: Combatting Cyber Harassment (essay)	*Key Skill* Identifying purpose and tone *Additional Skills* Understanding key vocabulary Using your knowledge Previewing Reading for details Reading for main ideas Identifying purpose and tone Synthesizing	Collocations for behavior Problem-solution collocations	
4 BUSINESS *Academic Disciplines* Entrepreneurship / Marketing / Social Media	Florida Teen Buys Houses	1: Starting Out Mobile (article) 2: Keeping Your Customers (article)	*Key Skill* Scanning to preview a text *Additional Skills* Using your knowledge Understanding key vocabulary Reading for main ideas Working out meaning Making inferences Synthesizing	Expressing contrast Business and marketing vocabulary	

CRITICAL THINKING	GRAMMAR FOR WRITING	WRITING	ON CAMPUS
Building support for an argument	Future real and unreal conditionals	*Academic Writing Skills* Paragraph structure and unity Impersonal statements *Rhetorical Mode* Argumentative *Writing Task* Make and support an argument for what to do with an aging but culturally or historically significant building. (essay)	*Study Skill* Staying organized with group projects
Determining and applying criteria	Nonidentifying relative clauses Appositives	*Academic Writing Skills* Structuring a summary-response essay Writing a conclusion *Rhetorical Mode* Summary-response *Writing Task* Summarize criteria and then analyze a logo in terms of that criteria. (essay)	*Life Skill* Building an academic resume
Determining the seriousness of a problem	Impersonal passive constructions Passive for continuity	*Academic Writing Skills* Writing about problems Writing about solutions *Rhetorical Mode* Problem-solution *Writing Task* Describe a problematic online behavior and explain what you think should be done to prevent or eliminate it. (essay)	*Research Skill* Identifying reliable online sources
Analyzing advantages and disadvantages	Reductions of subordinate clauses	*Academic Writing Skill* Writing about similarities and differences *Rhetorical Mode* Comparison and contrast *Writing Task* Compare and contrast (a) two products or services regarding their potential as a mobile business or (b) the appropriateness of loyalty programs and subscription services for a product or business. (report)	*Study Skill* Prioritizing your time

UNIT	WATCH AND LISTEN	READINGS	READING SKILLS	LANGUAGE DEVELOPMENT	
5 PSYCHOLOGY *Academic Disciplines* Experimental Science / History / Neuroscience	Interview with the Founders of IDEO	1: Mental Illness and Creative Genius: Is There a Connection? (article) 2: The Creative Mind (article)	*Key Skills* Using graphic organizers to take notes Interpreting quotes *Additional Skills* Understanding key vocabulary Previewing Reading for details Making inferences Predicting content using visuals Reading for main ideas Synthesizing	Experimental science terminology	
6 CAREERS *Academic Disciplines* Business / Education / Information Technology	Vocational Training	1: The Skills Gap (article) 2: What Is the Value of a College Education? (article)	*Key Skill* Interpreting graphical information *Additional Skills* Predicting content using visuals Understanding key vocabulary Reading for main ideas Reading for details Identifying purpose Making inferences Synthesizing	Complex noun phrases	
7 HEALTH SCIENCES *Academic Disciplines* Globalization / Medicine	Superbugs	1: Superbugs (article) 2: The Globalization of Infection (article)	*Key Skill* Recognizing discourse organization *Additional Skills* Using your knowledge Understanding key vocabulary Reading for main ideas Reading for details Working out meaning Making inferences Scanning to predict content Synthesizing	Verbs and verb phrases for causation Word families	
8 COLLABORATION *Academic Disciplines* Business / Human Resources / Sports Management	Office Space	1: The Value of Talent (article) 2: The Perfect Work Team (article)	*Key Skill* Using context clues to understand terminology and fixed expressions *Additional Skills* Previewing Understanding key vocabulary Reading for main ideas Summarizing Reading for details Using your knowledge Working out meaning	Language for hedging	

CRITICAL THINKING	GRAMMAR FOR WRITING	WRITING	ON CAMPUS
Annotation Finding points of synthesis across sources	Complex noun phrases with *what*	*Academic Writing Skills* Citing quoted material Writing an explanatory synthesis *Rhetorical Mode* Explanatory synthesis *Writing Task* What is creativity? Explain the current understanding of this concept, synthesizing information from different sources. (essay)	*Study Skill* Managing high volumes of reading
Analyzing information in graphs and other figures	Active vs. passive voice to discuss figures	*Academic Writing Skill* Making a claim *Rhetorical Mode* Argumentative *Writing Task* What is a good choice for a career path with a secure future? (essay with graphical support)	*Research Skill* Types of sources for research
Analyzing causes and effects	Cause and effect: logical connectors	*Academic Writing Skill* Writing about causes and effects *Rhetorical Mode* Cause and effect *Writing Task* Choose one infectious disease and discuss the factors that may have contributed to its development and spread or could do so in the future. (essay)	*Life Skill* Applying to a degree program
Understanding audience and purpose	Acknowledgment and concession	*Academic Writing Skill* Anticipating counterarguments *Rhetorical Mode* Argumentative *Writing Task* Present your recommendations for assembling and organizing an effective team for a particular business or collaborative group. (report)	*Communication Skill* The dynamics of group work

***Prism* is a five-level paired skills series for beginner- to advanced-level students of North American English.** Its five Reading and Writing and five Listening and Speaking levels are designed to equip students with the language and skills to be successful both inside and outside of the college classroom.

***Prism* uses a fresh approach to Critical Thinking based on a full integration of Bloom's taxonomy to help students become well-rounded critical thinkers.** The productive half of each unit begins with Critical Thinking. This section gives students the skills and tools they need to plan and prepare for success in their Speaking or Writing Task. Learners develop lower- and higher-order thinking skills, ranging from demonstrating knowledge and understanding to in-depth evaluation and analysis of content. Margin labels in the Critical Thinking sections highlight exercises that develop Bloom's concepts.

***Prism* focuses on the most relevant and important language for students of academic English based on comprehensive research.** Key vocabulary is taken from the General Service List, the Academic Word List, and the Cambridge English Corpus. The grammar selected is also corpus-informed.

***Prism* goes beyond language and critical thinking skills to teach students how to be successful, engaged college students both inside and outside of the classroom.** On Campus spreads at the end of each unit introduce students to communication, study, presentation, and life skills that will help them transition to life in North American community college and university programs.

***Prism* combines print and digital solutions for the modern student and program.** Online workbooks give students additional graded language and skills practice. Video resources are available to students and teachers in the same platform. Presentation Plus gives teachers modern tools to enhance their students' learning environment in the classroom.

***Prism* provides assessment resources for the busy teacher.** Photocopiable unit quizzes and answer keys are included in the Teacher's Manual, with downloadable PDF and Word versions available at Cambridge.org/prism and in the Resource tab of the Cambridge Learning Management System. A writing rubric for grading the Student's Book Writing Tasks and the Unit Quizzes is included in the Teacher's Manual.

SERIES LEVELS

Level	Description	CEFR Levels
Prism Intro	Beginner	A1
Prism 1	Low Intermediate	A2
Prism 2	Intermediate	B1
Prism 3	High Intermediate	B2
Prism 4	Advanced	C1

UNIT OPENER

Each unit opens with a striking two-page photo related to the topic, a Learning Objectives box, and an Activate Your Knowledge activity.

PURPOSE

- To introduce and generate interest in the unit topic with an engaging visual
- To set the learning objectives for the unit
- To make connections between students' background knowledge and the unit topic/theme

TEACHING SUGGESTIONS
PHOTO SPREAD

Lead an open class discussion on the connection between the unit opener photo and topic. Start off with questions like:

- *What is the first thing you notice in the photographs?*
- *What do you think of when you look at the photo?*
- *How is the photo connected to the unit title?*

ACTIVATE YOUR KNOWLEDGE

After students work in pairs to discuss the questions, have volunteers share with the class answers to questions that generated the most discussion.

You can also use the exercise to practice fluency. Instruct students to answer the questions as quickly as possible without worrying about creating grammatically correct sentences. Keep time and do not allow students more than 15–60 seconds per answer, depending on level and complexity of the question. You can then focus on accuracy when volunteers share their answers with the class.

WATCH AND LISTEN

Each unit includes a short authentic video from a respected news source that is related to the unit topic, along with exercises for students to do before, during, and after watching. The video can be played in the classroom or watched outside of class by students via the Cambridge LMS.

Note: A glossary defines above-level or specialized words that appear in the video and are essential for students to understand the main ideas so that teachers do not have to spend time pre-teaching or explaining this vocabulary while viewing.

PURPOSE

- To create a varied and dynamic learning experience
- To generate further interest in and discussion of the unit topic
- To build background knowledge and ideas on the topic
- To develop and practice key skills in prediction, comprehension, and discussion
- To personalize and give opinions on a topic

TEACHING SUGGESTIONS
PREPARING TO WATCH

Have students work in pairs to complete the Activating Your Knowledge exercise(s). Then have volunteers share their answers. Alternatively, students can complete this section on their own, and then compare answers with their partners.

For a livelier class discussion, look at the visuals from the Predicting Content Using Visuals exercise(s) as a class and answer the questions together.

WHILE WATCHING

Watch the video twice, once while students listen for main ideas and once while they listen for key details. After each viewing, facilitate a discussion of students' answers and clarify any confusion. If some students still have trouble with comprehension, suggest that they watch the video again at home or during a computer lab session.

DISCUSSION

Have students work in pairs or small groups to answer the discussion questions. Have students compare their answers with another pair or group. Then have volunteers share their answers with the class. If possible, expand on their answers by making connections between their answers and the video content. For example: *That's an interesting perspective. How is it similar to what the speaker in the video mentioned? How is it different?*
For writing practice, have students write responses to the questions for homework.

READING

The first half of each unit focuses on the receptive skill of reading. Each unit includes two reading passages that provide different angles, viewpoints, and/or genres related to the unit topic.

READING 1

Reading 1 includes a reading passage on an academic topic. It provides information on the unit topic, and it gives students exposure to and practice with language and reading skills while helping them begin to generate ideas for their Writing Task.

PREPARING TO READ
PURPOSE

- To prepare students to understand the content of the reading
- To introduce, review, and/or practice key pre-reading skills
- To introduce and build key academic and topical vocabulary for the reading and for the unit Writing Task

TEACHING SUGGESTIONS

Encourage students to complete the pre-reading activities in this section in pairs or groups. This will promote a high level of engagement. Once students have completed the activities, check for understanding and offer any clarification.
Encourage or assign your students to keep a vocabulary notebook for new words. This should include new key vocabulary words, parts of speech, definitions (in the students' own words), and contextual sentences. To extend the vocabulary activity in this section, ask students to find synonyms, antonyms, or related terms for the vocabulary items they just practiced. These can then be added to their vocabulary notebooks.
Key vocabulary exercises can also be assigned ahead of time so that you can focus on the reading content and skills in class.
If time permits, have students scan Reading 1 for the key vocabulary just practiced in bold and read the sentences with each term. This will provide additional pre-reading scaffolding.

WHILE READING
PURPOSE

- To introduce, review, and/or practice key academic reading skills
- To practice reading comprehension and annotation skills
- To see and understand key vocabulary in a natural academic context
- To provide information and stimulate ideas on an academic topic
- To help students become more efficient readers

TEACHING SUGGESTIONS

Have students work in pairs or small groups to complete the activities. Students should always be prepared to support their answers from the text, so encourage them to annotate the text as they complete the activities. After students complete the activities, have volunteers share their answers with the class, along with support from the text. If necessary, facilitate clarification by referring back to the text yourself. Use guided questions to help with understanding. For example: *Take a moment to review the final sentences of Paragraph 2. What words discuss a problem?*

READING BETWEEN THE LINES

PURPOSE

- To introduce, expand on, and/or practice key reading skills related to students' ability to infer meaning, text type, purpose, audience, etc.
- To introduce, review, and/or practice key critical thinking skills applied to content from the reading passage

TEACHING SUGGESTIONS

Have students complete the activities in pairs or small groups and share their answers with the class. It is particularly important for students to be able to support their answers using the text at this point. Encourage students to work out any partial or wrong answers by asking a series of clear, guided questions like: *You thought the author meant ... What about this sentence in the reading? What information does it give us? Does this sentence change your mind about your answer?*"

After checking answers, survey students on what they found most challenging in the section. Then have students read the text again for homework, making additional annotations and notes on the challenging skills and content to be shared at the beginning of the next class or in an online forum.

DISCUSSION

PURPOSE

- To give students the opportunity to discuss and offer opinions about what they read
- To think critically about the content of the reading
- To further personalize the topic and issues in Reading 1

TEACHING SUGGESTIONS

Give students three to five minutes to discuss and jot down notes for their answers before discussing them in pairs or small groups. Monitor student groups, taking notes on common mistakes. Then, survey the students on their favorite questions and have groups volunteer to share these answers. You can provide oral or written feedback on common mistakes at the end of the section.

READING 2

Reading 2 is a reading passage on the unit topic from a different angle and often in a different format than Reading 1. It gives students additional exposure to and practice with language and reading skills while helping them generate and refine ideas for their Writing Task. It generally includes rhetorical elements that serve as a structured model for the Writing Task.

PREPARING TO READ

PURPOSE

- To prepare students to understand the content of the reading
- To introduce, review, and/or practice key pre-reading skills
- To introduce and build key academic and topical vocabulary for the reading and for the unit Writing Task

TEACHING SUGGESTIONS

As with Reading 1, encourage students to complete the activities in this section in pairs or small groups to promote a high level of engagement. Circulate among students at this time, taking notes of common areas of difficulty. Once students have completed the activities, check for understanding and offer clarification, paying particular attention to any problem areas you noted.

If you wish to extend the vocabulary activity in this section, elicit other word forms of the key vocabulary. Students can add these word forms to their vocabulary notebooks.

WHILE READING

PURPOSE

- To introduce, review, and/or practice key academic reading skills
- To practice reading comprehension and annotation skills
- To see and understand key vocabulary in a natural academic context
- To provide information and stimulate ideas on an academic topic
- To help students become more efficient readers
- To model aspects or elements of the Writing Task

TEACHING SUGGESTIONS

As with Reading 1, have students work in pairs or small groups to complete the activities. Encourage them to annotate the reading so that they are prepared to support their answers from the text. Elicit answers and explanations from the class. Remember to facilitate clarification by referring back to the text yourself, using clear, guided questions to help with understanding.

Alternatively, separate the class into multiple groups, and assign a paragraph or section of the reading to each groups. (Students should skim the rest of the passage not assigned to them.) Set a time limit for reading. Then do the exercises as a class, with each group responsible for answering and explaining the items that fall within their paragraph or section of the text.

READING BETWEEN THE LINES

PURPOSE

- To introduce, expand on, and/or practice key reading skills related to students' ability to infer meaning, text type, purpose, audience, etc.
- To introduce, review, and/or practice key critical thinking skills applied to content from the reading passage

TEACHING SUGGESTIONS

For Making Inferences activities, have students work in pairs to answer the questions. Instruct pairs to make notes in the margins about the clues from the text they use to answer the questions. Then have pairs meet up with other pairs to compare their clues. Have volunteers share their clues and answers with the class.

For other activity types, such as Recognizing Genre or Distinguishing Fact from Opinion, have students work in pairs and then share their answers with the class as before. Then promote deeper engagement with guided questions like:

- *How is an essay different from a newspaper article?*
- *What are common features of a* [text type]?
- *What words in the sentence tell you that you are reading an opinion and not a fact?*
- *Can you say more about what x means?*

DISCUSSION

PURPOSE

- To personalize and expand on the ideas and content of Reading 2
- To practice synthesizing the content of the unit reading passages

Before students discuss the questions in this section the first time, introduce the key skill of synthesis. Start by defining synthesis (combining and analyzing ideas from multiple sources). Stress its importance in higher education: in college or graduate school, students will be asked to synthesize ideas from a wide range of sources, to think critically about them, to make connections among them, and to add their own ideas. Note: you may need to review this information periodically with your class.

Have students answer the questions in pairs or small groups, and then ask for volunteers to share their answers with the class. Facilitate the discussion, encouraging students to make connections between Reading 1 and Reading 2. If applicable, ask students to relate the content of the unit video to this section. This is also a good context in which to introduce the Writing Task at the beginning of the Critical Thinking section and to have students consider how the content of the reading passages relates to the prompt.

To extend this activity beyond discussion, write the connections students make on the board, and have students take notes. Students can then use their notes to write sentences or a paragraph(s) describing how the ideas in all the sources discussed are connected.

LANGUAGE DEVELOPMENT

Each unit includes academic language relevant to the unit topic and readings and useful for the unit Writing Task. The focus of this section is on vocabulary and/or grammar.

PURPOSE

- To recycle and expand on vocabulary that appears in Reading 1 or Reading 2
- To focus and expand on grammar that appears in Reading 1 or Reading 2
- To expose students to additional corpus-informed, research-based language for the unit topic and level
- To practice language and structures that students can use in the Writing Task

TEACHING SUGGESTIONS

For grammar points, review the Language Box as a class and facilitate answers to any unclear sections. Alternatively, have students review it in pairs and allow time for questions. Then have students work in pairs to complete the accompanying activities. Review students' answers, allowing time for any clarification.

For vocabulary points, have students complete the exercises in pairs. Then, review answers and allow time for any clarification. To extend this activity, have students create sentences using each term and/or make a list of synonyms, antonyms, or related words and phrases for each term. Students should also add relevant language to their vocabulary notebooks. For homework, have students annotate the readings in the unit, underlining or highlighting any language covered in this section.

WRITING

The second half of each unit focuses on the productive skill of writing. It begins with the prompt for the Writing Task and systematically equips students with the grammar and skills to plan for, prepare, and execute the task successfully.

CRITICAL THINKING

PURPOSE

- To introduce the Writing Task
- To notice and analyze features of Reading 2 related to the Writing Task
- To help generate, develop, and organize ideas for the Writing Task
- To teach and practice the lower-order critical thinking skills of remembering, understanding, and applying knowledge through practical brainstorming and organizational activities
- To teach and practice the higher-order critical thinking skills of analyzing, evaluating, and creating in order to prepare students for success in the Writing Task and, more generally, in the college classroom

Encourage students to work through this section collaboratively in pairs or small groups to promote a high level of engagement. Facilitate their learning and progress by circulating and checking in on students as they work through this section. If time permits, have groups exchange and evaluate one another's work.

Note: Students will often be directed back to this section to review, revise, and expand on their initial ideas and notes for the Writing Task.

GRAMMAR FOR WRITING

PURPOSE

- To introduce and practice grammar that is relevant to the Writing Task
- To introduce and practice grammar that often presents trouble for students at this level of academic writing

TEACHING SUGGESTIONS

Review any Skills boxes in this section as a class, allowing time to answer questions and clarify points of confusion. Then have students work on the activities in pairs or small groups, before eliciting answers as a class.

ACADEMIC WRITING SKILLS

PURPOSE

- To present and practice academic writing skills needed to be successful in college or graduate school
- To focus on specific language and skills relevant to the Writing Task

TEACHING SUGGESTIONS

Have students read any Skills boxes on their own. Check understanding by asking guided questions like:

- *What do you notice about the parallel structure examples?*
- *What are some other examples of parallel structure?*
- *How would you describe parallel structure based on the information and examples you just read?*

Provide clarification as necessary, offering and eliciting more examples. Have students find examples in the unit readings if possible.

Students can work in pairs to complete the exercises and then share their answers with the class. Alternatively, assign exercises for homework.

WRITING TASK

PURPOSE

- To work collaboratively in preparation for the Writing Task
- To revisit, revise, and expand on work done in the Critical Thinking section
- To provide an opportunity for students to synthesize the language, skills, and ideas presented and generated in the unit
- To help students plan, draft, revise, and edit their writing

TEACHING SUGGESTIONS

Depending on time and class level, students can complete the preparation activities for homework or in class. If conducted in class, have students work on their own to complete the Plan section. They can then share their plans in pairs. Give students time to revise their plans based on feedback from their partners.

Depending on time, students can write their first drafts at home or in class. Encourage students to refer to the Task Checklist before and after writing their first drafts. The checklist can also be used in a peer review of first drafts in class.

Note: At this stage, encourage students to focus on generating and organizing their ideas, and answering the prompt, rather than perfecting their grammar, which they will focus on during the Edit stage using the Language Checklist.

Even with a peer review, it is important to provide written feedback for your students, either on their first or second drafts. When doing so, look for common mistakes in student writing. Select at least one problem sentence or area from each student's draft, and conduct an edit correction exercise either as a class or in an online discussion forum. You can also select and review a well-written sentence from each draft to serve as models and to provide positive reinforcement.

ON CAMPUS

Each unit concludes with a unique spread that teaches students concepts and skills that go beyond traditional reading and writing academic skills.

PURPOSE

- To familiarize students with all aspects of the North American college experience
- To enable students to interact and participate successfully in the college classroom
- To prepare students to navigate typical North American college campus life

TEACHING SUGGESTIONS

PREPARING TO READ

Begin with an open discussion by asking students what they know about the topic.
For example:

- *What is a study plan?*
- *Have you ever written an email to a teacher or professor?*
- *How do college students choose a major?*
- *What is a virtual classroom?*

You can also write the question on the board and assign as pair work, and have students share their answers with the class.

WHILE READING

Have students read the text and complete the accompanying activities. Have them read again and check their work. You can extend these activities by asking the following questions:

- *What did you find most interesting in this reading passage?*
- *What did you understand more clearly during the second reading?*
- *Who do you think wrote the text? Why?*

PRACTICE

Have students read any Skills boxes silently. Give them two minutes to discuss the information with partners before they complete the exercises. Elicit from some volunteers how the exercises practice what they read in the text.

REAL-WORLD APPLICATION

Depending on time, you may want to assign the activities in this section as homework. Having students collaborate on these real-world tasks either inside or outside of the classroom simulates a common practice in college and graduate school. At the beginning of the week you can set up a schedule so that several student groups present their work during class throughout the week.

To extend this section, assign small related research projects, as applicable. For example, have students research and report on three websites with information on choosing a college major.

PRISM WRITING TASK RUBRIC

CATEGORY	CRITERIA	SCORE
Content and Development	• Writing completes the task and fully answers the prompt. • Content is meaningful and interesting. • Main points and ideas are fully developed with good support and logic.	

Organization	• Writing is well-organized and follows the conventions of academic writing:
	  • Paragraph – topic sentence, supporting details, concluding sentence
	  • Essay – introduction with thesis, body paragraphs, conclusion
	• Rhetorical mode(s) used is appropriate to the Writing Task.	

Coherence, Clarity, and Unity	• Sentences within a paragraph flow logically with appropriate transitions; paragraphs within an essay flow logically with appropriate transitions. • Sentences and ideas are clear and make sense to the reader. • All sentences in a paragraph relate to the topic sentence; all paragraphs in an essay relate to the thesis.	
Vocabulary	• Vocabulary, including expressions and transition language, is accurate, appropriate, and varied. • Writing shows mastery of unit key vocabulary and Language Development.	
Grammar and Writing Skills	• Grammar is accurate, appropriate, and varied. • Writing shows mastery of unit Grammar for Writing and Language Development. • Sentence types are varied and used appropriately. • Level of formality shows an understanding of audience and purpose. • Mechanics (capitalization, punctuation, indentation, and spelling) are strong. • Writing shows mastery of unit Academic Writing Skills.	

How well does the response meet the criteria?	Recommended Score
At least 90%	20
At least 75%	15
At least 60%	10
At least 50%	5
Less than 50%	0
Total Score Possible per Section	20
Total Score Possible	100

Feedback:

STUDENT'S BOOK ANSWER KEY

UNIT 1
ACTIVATE YOUR KNOWLEDGE

page 15
Answers will vary.

WATCH AND LISTEN

Exercises 1 and 2 page 16
Answers will vary.

Exercise 3 page 17
3 How a CD is manufactured, how it has been handled, and how it has been stored, all impact its longevity.

Exercise 4 page 17
Answers will vary. Possible answers:
1 This will help them better understand how to keep them safe for posterity.
2 CDs are cooked in chambers by manipulating the humidity and the temperature.
3 Do not put fancy labels on them, do not use Sharpies, and write only in the small center region.

Exercises 5 and 6 page 17
Answers will vary.

READING 1

Exercise 1 page 18
Answers will vary.

Exercise 2 page 19
Answers will vary.

Exercise 3 page 19
a vulnerable
b practice
c prompt
d recover
e capacity
f deliberate
g memorabilia
h emerge

Exercise 4 page 21
1 c
2 If current practices continue, future generations may not have access to the digital record of our lives and our world.

Exercise 5 page 21
1 (a) A box of memorabilia, including floppy discs and VHS tapes, is found in the attic of an old house with a label that says, "Records and early videos of Bill Gates (1975–1985)."

(b) [A]n envelope labeled "bank records" in your grandmother's desk. Inside the envelope, there is an old CD marked with the date 1998, your great-grandfather's name, and the words "all overseas bank accounts."
2 b, c

Exercise 6 page 21
1 F 2 T 3 T 4 DNS 5 F 6 F

Exercise 7 page 22
Answers will vary. Possible answers:
1 They would be excited to have discovered materials they thought were lost. Then they might realize that they had no way to access the information.
2 We don't have a lot of information about the Dark Ages, so we don't fully understand what happened during that time.
3 *Bit rot* might mean the loss of digitally held information.
4 Interactive apps and websites go out of date very quickly.

Exercise 8 page 22
Answers will vary.

READING 2

Exercise 1 page 22
Answers will vary. Possible answers:
1 both texts are letters
2 members of the county board
3 residents of the neighborhood who have formed organizations
4 what to do with the Cook County Hospital

Exercise 2 page 23
1 c
2 a
3 c
4 b
5 a
6 a
7 a
8 b

Exercise 3 **page 25**
1 a
2 *What this neighborhood needs is an up-to-date, green structure that will provide much-needed housing and retail space.*
3 b
4 *Our group's proposal for renovation of the hospital site and building will allow it to continue to serve the community by providing affordable housing, medical clinics, a school, and a community center—resources that we badly need.*

Exercise 4 page 25

1 a, d

2 Our experts agree that updating this one hundred-year-old building to meet modern safety standards would actually be more expensive than starting from scratch. / Just as important, construction of these structures, and the businesses that will be located in them, will provide good jobs for people in the community.

3 a, b, e

4 In fact, renovating an existing structure can cost about $25 per square foot less than even the most basic new construction, while preserving the beauty of the original building. / Our group's proposal for renovation of the hospital site and building will allow it to continue to serve the community by providing affordable housing, medical clinics, a school, and a community center—resources that we badly need. / New construction almost always has a more serious environmental impact because it requires the use of all new materials.

Exercise 5 page 26

Answers will vary. Possible Answers:

1 The people behind the New Neighborhood Group are those that moved into the neighborhood more recently. Their goals are to update the neighborhood.

2 The people behind the Citizens Neighborhood are people who have lived in the neighborhood for a long time. Their goals are to preserve the buildings in the neighborhood.

3 Cook County Hospital was compared to the Statue of Liberty because it welcomed people of all backgrounds and classes.

4 It means that it has less environmental impact since it doesn't need new materials.

Exercise 6 page 26

Answers will vary.

LANGUAGE DEVELOPMENT

Exercise 1 page 27

1 out of date
2 It's about time for
3 slowly but surely
4 at the turn of the century
5 At one time / At the turn of the century
6 in a flash / in the blink of an eye
7 for the time being
8 Over the past / Over the last
9 up to date

Exercise 2 page 27

Answers will vary.

Exercise 3 page 28

1 long-term
2 low-income
3 turn of the century
4 one-way
5 well known
6 single-family
7 energy efficient
8 fast-growing

Exercise 4 page 28

Answers will vary.

CRITICAL THINKING

Exercise 1 page 29

1 P
2 P
3 NC
4 P
5 P
6 P
7 NC
8 NC

Exercise 2 page 30

Factor	Fact
environmental impact	1, 3, 5
community impact	2, 4
economic impact	6, 7, 8

Exercises 3 and 4 page 30

Answers will vary.

GRAMMAR FOR WRITING

Exercise 1 page 31

1 a
2 b
3 a
4 b

Exercise 2 page 31

Answers will vary.

ACADEMIC WRITING SKILLS

Exercise 1 pages 31–32

1 a
2 b
3 a
4 a

Exercise 2 pages 32–33

1 unified
2 not unified: *They cannot make major changes that affect the appearance of their home without the approval of a committee that is in charge of the district.*

3 unified

4 not unified: *It offers a $50,000 annual book prize for a work on U.S. history. It is the oldest museum in New York.*

Exercise 3 pages 33
Answers will vary. Possible answers:

1 City leaders did not act responsible when they voted to allow construction on park land.

2 Reusing and recycling resources is always better that using up additional resources.

3 Since a convention center would provide both jobs and revenue, it would be an incredible benefit for this city and its citizens.

4 We are telling low-income homebuyers to stay away when we designate the neighborhood a historic area.

5 Placing this building on the register of historic places has the potential to draw tourists who are interested in architectural and cultural history and is, therefore, a step in the right direction.

ON CAMPUS

Exercise 1 page 36
Answers will vary.

Exercise 2 page 36

1 a file-sharing program
2 has easy access to and is comfortable with
3 sharing files
4 topic
5 change it completely; date, writer's initials, or number
6 move them

Exercises 3–5 page 37
Answers will vary.

UNIT 2
ACTIVATE YOUR KNOWLEDGE

page 39
Answers will vary.

WATCH AND LISTEN

Exercises 1 and 2 page 40
Answers will vary.

Exercise 3 page 41

2 Many corporations today use Helvetica because it communicates a clear message.

Exercise 4 page 41

1 zany hand lettering, exclamation points
2 accessible, transparent, and accountable

Exercise 5 and 6 page 41
Answers will vary.

READING 1

Exercise 1 page 42
Answers will vary.

Exercise 2 page 42

a contemporary
b human rights
c subsequent
d donation
e criteria
f retain
g appropriate
h devoted to

Exercise 3 page 42

b

Exercise 4 page 45

I. A. 1. Example: *Answers will vary.*
I. A. 2. Example: *Answers will vary.*
I. B. Unique
I. B. 1. Example: IKEA
I. B. 2. Example: *Answers will vary.*
I. C. curiosity
I. C. 1. Example: UNIQLO
I. C. 2. Example: *Answers will vary.*
II. Flexible
II. A. time
II. A. 1. Example: Apple
II. A. 2. Example: *Answers will vary.*
II. B. across space
II. B. 1. Example: Twitter or Facebook
II. B. 2. Can be recognized from a distance
II. B. 2. Example: *Answers will vary.*
III. Tells a story
III. A. Conveys company's identity
    Example: Toys-R-Us or FedEx
III. B. Evokes emotional response
    Example: WWF

Exercise 5 page 46
Answers will vary. Possible answers:
odd combination of letters; Odd arrangement of letters; letters all in caps

Exercise 6 page 46
Answers will vary.

Exercise 7 page 46
Answers will vary. Possible answers:
a; contains the word "bank" in it in blue, so it stands out; includes image of a key that indicates company is secure and safe

Exercise 8 page 46
Answers will vary.

READING 2

Exercise 1 page 47
Answers will vary.

Exercise 2 page 47
1 b
2 a
3 c
4 c
5 a
6 b
7 c
8 b

Exercise 3 page 49
a, b, d

Exercise 4 page 49
1 f
2 c
3 d
4 b
5 a
6 e

Exercise 5 page 50
Answers will vary. Possible answers:
I companies expand / change products they sell; e.g., Xerox = photocopiers to bigger document technology; neg. associations with companies; e.g., Kentucky Fried Chicken = unhealthy fried food; British Petroleum = gas bad for climate
II young entrepreneurs age; e.g., Spotify = sound waves. Snapchat = no silly face on ghost
III people resistant to change; sometimes don't like new logo; e.g., Coca Cola dropped orange logo, people hated it, so went back to old logo
IV smaller devices and platforms need smaller logos; e.g., Airbnb and PayPal = drop names, simpler graphic

Exercise 6 page 50
a, b, c, d, e

Exercise 7 page 50
Answers will vary.

LANGUAGE DEVELOPMENT

Exercise 1 page 51
b mixed
c mixed
d negative
e positive
f negative

Exercise 2 page 51
1 aroused suspicion
2 provoked controversy / provoked outrage / stirred up opposition / evoked emotions / evoked memories / aroused anger
3 aroused, interest / generated, interest / generated, excitement
4 inspires confidence / stirs up opposition / provokes outrage
5 provoked, response
6 evoke, memories / evoke, emotions

Exercise 3 page 51
Answers will vary.

Exercise 4 page 52
Answers will vary. Some examples:
1 Companies and other organizations often use logos to promote their identity and increase public recognition.
2 Often companies' logos reflect their names, origins, and products so that consumers can connect logos to companies.
3 Color is really important in a logo because it helps consumers distinguish between similar logos.
4 Sports teams earn a lot of money from logos placed on clothing, souvenirs, and other merchandising products.

Exercise 5 page 52
Answers will vary.

CRITICAL THINKING

Exercise 1 page 53
Answers will vary. Possible answers:
1 It's clear and simple.
2 It's unique.
3 It's flexible and adaptable.
4 It conveys a message / evokes a response.
5 It's appropriate for the organization it represents.

Exercises 2 and 3 page 53
Answers will vary.

GRAMMAR FOR WRITING

Exercise 1 page 54
Answers will vary. Possible answers:
1 Apple's logo, which was once rainbow colored, has been redesigned several times in the past 40 years.
2 The letters in the logo for FedEx, which is a delivery service company, form an arrow moving forward.
3 Predrag Stakić, who is a Serbian designer, won an international competition for a logo that features images of a bird and a hand.
4 Rebranding, which is a process that can revive interest in a company's products, is only one of many options available to the marketing department.
5 High-tech companies, which often have very young founders, have realized that they need to reconsider and revise their logos.

Exercise 2 page 55

1 McDonald's logo, the golden arches, has achieved international recognition as a symbol of fast food.
2 The design of logos, a company's public face, requires careful thought and preparation before they are released.
3 Rupert Murdoch, a media mogul, has announced he will turn over his media empire to his son next year. / Media mogul Rupert Murdoch has announced he will turn over his media empire to his son next year.
4 Microsoft, a software giant, has lost some of its market share to Google in the past five years, and the trend continues with the latest software release. / Software giant Microsoft has lost some of its market share to Google in the past five years, and the trend continues with the latest software release.
5 *Answers will vary.*
6 *Answers will vary.*

ACADEMIC WRITING SKILLS

Exercises 1–3 page 56
Answers will vary.

Exercise 4 page 57
Answers will vary. Possible answers:

1 "What Makes a Successful Logo?" main idea: A successful logo captures a company's identity and message in a way that is memorable and pleasing to look at.
"Rebranding and Logos" main idea: Rebranding is a way a company can revitalize its image and message in order to appeal to today's customers.
2 Main idea: *convey an immediately recognizable and unmistakable message of human rights.*
New idea: Serbian designer, Predrag Stakić's logo, which combines the images of a bird and a human hand.
3 Main idea: *the process can inject new energy into a brand*
New idea: New logos can be expensive. They can also be risky.

ON CAMPUS

Exercise 1 page 60
Answers will vary.

Exercise 2 page 60

Do ...	Don't ...
include unpaid work experience ask someone to read it provide your email address include activities that aren't at school provide dates of everything	abbreviate include your birthday exaggerate provide your social security number be very detailed include small jobs

Exercise 3 page 60
Answers will vary.

Exercises 4 and 5 page 61
Answers will vary.

UNIT 3
ACTIVATE YOUR KNOWLEDGE

page 63
Answers will vary.

WATCH AND LISTEN

Exercises 1 and 2 page 64
Answers will vary.

Exercise 3 page 65

1 F; None of the cases were a result of a breach in Apple's security.
2 T
3 F; The people who posted the photos may be liable, and could be charged.
4 T
5 T

Exercise 4 page 65

1 user names, passwords, and security questions
2 mobile phones, computer, backup systems
3 Computer Fraud and Abuse Act; could be 5 years

Exercises 5 and 6 page 65
Answers will vary.

READING 1

Exercise 1 page 66

a abusive
b disturbing
c guarantee
d validity
e anonymous
f violate
g humiliation
h withdraw

Exercise 2 page 66
Answers will vary. Possible answers:

1 cyber: of or having to do with the Internet
harassment: hostile intimidation or pressure
2 *Answers will vary. Possible answer:*
Intimidating or pressuring someone online through email and social media.

Exercise 3 page 67
Answers will vary.

Exercise 4 page 67

1 SD, 5
2 MI, 3
3 SD, 2
4 MI, 4
5 MI, 5
6 MI, 1
7 SD, 4
8 MI, 2
9 SD, 1
10 SD, 3

Exercise 5 page 67

Answers will vary. Possible answers:
I. Cyber harassment takes many forms.
  A. Cyber harassment includes physical threats.
II. Many Internet users experience cyber harassment.
  A. Forty percent of Internet users have experienced some form of cyber harassment.
III. Trolls engage in disruptive behavior for a variety of reasons.
  A. Trolls harass other Internet users because they enjoy causing pain.
IV. It is difficult to stop cyber harassment.
  A. Limiting offensive speech may be considered a violation of the right to free speech.
V. Victims of cyber harassment often do not get a lot of support.
  A. Complaints about cyber harassment by victims are sometimes considered too dramatic.

Exercise 6 page 69

1 c
2 a
3 *Answers will vary.*

Exercise 7 page 69

Answers will vary.

READING 2

Exercise 1 page 70
Answers will vary.

Exercise 2 pages 70–71

1 c
2 b
3 c
4 a
5 a
6 b
7 a
8 c

Exercise 3 page 71

a 2
b 4
c 5
d 1
e 3

Exercise 4 page 71

group	actions
online gaming communities	create barriers to bad behaviors, such as removing chat function establish player rating system
Twitter	add "report abuse" button
Google	do research to identify abusers using an algorithm
federal and state governments	update laws to cover stalking and threats on the Internet

Exercise 5 page 73

1 b, c, d, e
2 b
3 *Answers will vary.*

Exercise 6 page 73
Answers will vary.

LANGUAGE DEVELOPMENT

Exercise 1 page 74

1 take responsibility
2 built a reputation
3 experienced abuse
4 exhibit, behavior
5 suffer pain
6 lose confidence

Exercise 2 page 74
Answers will vary.

Exercise 3 page 75
Answers will vary.

CRITICAL THINKING

Exercises 1 and 2 page 76
Answers will vary.

GRAMMAR FOR WRITING

Exercise 1 page 77

1 The figures are believed to underestimate the size of the problem. / It is believed the figures underestimate the size of the problem.
2 Trolls are claimed to be responsible for the most abusive forms of cyber harassment. / It is claimed that trolls are responsible for the most abusive forms of cyber harassment.
3 Victims of online harassment are expected to speak out against their abusers. / It is expected that victims of online harassment will speak out against their abusers.
4 Self-regulation is understood to be the best way to control bad behavior. / It is understood that self-regulation is the best way to control bad behavior.
5 "Just ignore it" is considered to be sensible advice to victims of online harassment.
6 It has been argued that these problems will require a legal solution.

Exercise 2 page 77
Answers will vary.

Exercise 3 page 78

1 Although the stalker had been harassing students for weeks, he was not caught until yesterday.
2 A full year after the plane disappeared over the Indian Ocean, pieces of it were seen by the crew of a fishing boat over 25 miles from shore.
3 Coffee is one of Brazil's most important crops. Most of it is grown in the area along the Atlantic coast.
4 One week after Congress passed a bill to make cyber harassment illegal, it was signed into law by the president.
5 Polar bears and some other Arctic animals are in danger of extinction. Their habitat has been drastically reduced by climate change.

Exercise 4 page 78
Answers will vary. Possible answer:
Identity theft is a growing problem. It occurs when someone uses your personal information to open bank accounts, borrow money, and make purchases. This crime was reported by almost 17 million people last year. The elderly are especially likely to become victims. Over 2.6 million older people were targeted in 2014. Stolen credit cards were the most common source of identity theft. Unfortunately, they are not usually recovered.

ACADEMIC WRITING SKILLS

Exercise 1 page 79
1 S 2 F 3 O 4 F 5 E 6 E 7 O 8 S

Exercise 2 page 79
Answers will vary.

Exercise 3 page 80
1 R
2 S
3 G
4 G
5 S
6 R

Exercise 4 page 80
Answers will vary.

ON CAMPUS

Exercise 1 page 84
Answers will vary.

Exercise 2 page 84
1 b
2 f
3 d
4 a
5 e
6 c

Exercise 3 page 85
2, 4, 5, 6

Exercise 4 page 85
Answers will vary.

UNIT 4
ACTIVATE YOUR KNOWLEDGE

page 87
Answers will vary.

WATCH AND LISTEN

Exercises 1 and 2 page 88
Answers will vary.

Exercise 3 page 89
1, 2, 3, 4

Exercise 4 page 89
Answers will vary. Possible answers:
1 She made $6,000 which helped her purchase a $12,000 home.
2/3 Her mother is a realtor, and legally owns the properties, and will sign them over to her when she is 18.
4 She collects rent, shops for materials, and takes stock of her next project.

Exercises 5 and 6 page 89
Answers will vary.

READING 1

Exercise 1 page 90
Students make predictions here, but the actual answers are as follows, for reference:
1 F
2 T
3 F
4 T
5 T
6 F

Exercise 2 page 90
1 fluctuated
2 proposition
3 aspiring
4 outweigh
5 component
6 transition
7 broke even
8 revenue

Exercise 3 page 91
1 $20,000–$30,000
2 boxing gym
3 food trucks, flowers, shoes, clothes, hair styling, dog grooming, repair of high-tech devices
4 12%
5 weather, fluctuating gas prices, parking
6 $857 million

Exercise 4 page 91
1 N
2 M
3 Y
4 N
5 Y
6 N

Exercise 5 page 91
Answers will vary. Possible answer:
Mobile businesses are a good first step into the retail market.

Exercise 6 page 93
1 b
2 e
3 g
4 c
5 a
6 d
7 h
8 f

Exercises 7 and 8 page 93
Answers will vary.

READING 2

Exercise 1 page 93
Answers will vary.

Exercise 2 page 94
1 b
2 a
3 a
4 c
5 a
6 b
7 a
8 c

Exercise 3 page 96
b, c, f

Exercise 4 page 96
1 simple
2 attainable
3 valuable
4 consumers
5 airlines
6 convenience
7 desires
8 decisions
9 $1,500
10 $625

Exercise 5 page 96
Answers will vary.

Exercise 6 page 97
Answers will vary.

LANGUAGE DEVELOPMENT

Exercise 1 page 98
1 b
2 a
3 c
4 a
5 b

Exercise 2 page 98
1 on a small scale
2 start-up costs / utilities
3 utilities / start-up costs
4 breaks even
5 turn a profit / generates revenue
6 brick-and-mortar
7 track record
8 generate revenue
9 marketing tools

CRITICAL THINKING

Exercise 1 page 99
Answers will vary. Possible answers:

advantages	disadvantages
lower risk lower cost • startup • utility • overhead gradual start for those who don't know much about business can take product directly to customers a truck is its own advertisement	parking gas prices are unpredictable small size limits activity laws that restrict mobile businesses not everything works in a truck

Exercise 2 page 99
Answers will vary.

Exercise 3 page 100
Answers will vary. Possible answers:

loyalty programs	subscription services
good for both high-cost and low-cost items	good for products that offer a little bit of luxury
good for a single product (e.g., coffee) or a whole business (e.g., a supermarket)	good for products with "too many" choices
good for promoting long-term customer relationships	good for products where customers would appreciate expert advice

Exercise 4 page 100
Answers will vary.

GRAMMAR FOR WRITING

Exercise 1 pages 101–102
Answers may vary. Possible answers:

1 <u>Surprised by the rude behavior of the sales assistant</u>, Karina never returned to the store.
Because Katrina was surprised by the rude behavior of the sales assistant, she never returned to the store.

2 <u>While working on a food truck</u>, Kwan developed enough experience to start his own business.
While Kwan was working on a food truck, he developed enough experience to start his own business.

3 <u>Looking at the message board at the community center</u>, Isabelle got an idea for a new mobile business—a dog-washing service at the park!
While Isabelle was looking at the message board at the community center, she got an idea for a new mobile business—a dog-washing service at the park!

4 <u>Once discovered by the food reporter for a local foodie site</u>, the Tina's Tacos truck had more business than its owners could handle.
After Tina's Tacos was discovered by the food reporter for a loal foodie site, it had more business than its owners could handle.

5 <u>Encouraged by the good reviews of her friends</u>, Alya joined a subscription program for natural beauty products.
Alya was encouraged by the good reviews of her friends, so she joined a subscription program for natural beauty products.

Exercise 2 page 102
Answers may vary. Possible answers:

1 Hurt by the negative response to her cooking, Claudia decided not to open a restaurant.
2 Researching marketing tools, David was surprised to learn about the inconsistent track record of loyalty programs.
3 Unless embraced by a large number of customers, loyalty programs are not very effective marketing tools.
4 Worried about start-up costs, the Hernández brothers decided to begin their business online.
5 If taken seriously, this advice can dramatically improve a company's chances of success.

ACADEMIC WRITING SKILLS

Exercise 1 page 103
1 block; point-by-point
2 *Answers will vary.*

Exercise 2 page 104
1 b
2 *Answers will vary.*
3 d; points out Choi's popularity and success in food truck industry, but acknowledges the value of his restaurant experience

ON CAMPUS

Exercise 1 page 108
Answers will vary.

Exercise 2 page 108
1 G
2 B
3 G
4 G
5 B
6 B

Exercise 3 page 108
Answers will vary.

Exercise 4 page 109
Answers will vary.

UNIT 5
ACTIVATE YOUR KNOWLEDGE

page 111
Answers will vary.

WATCH AND LISTEN

Exercises 1 and 2 page 112
Answers will vary.

Exercise 3 page 113
1 b
2 a
3 a

Exercise 4 page 113
Answers will vary. Possible answers:
1 reengineer / improve
2 discovered / found / learned
3 opting out / giving up / believing they are not creative
4 fostered / practiced
5 empathy / an understanding
6 breakthrough / innovative / great

Exercises 5 and 6 page 113
Answers will vary.

READING 1

Exercise 1 page 114
1 suppress
2 norm
3 skeptical
4 reject
5 notion
6 intriguing
7 labeled
8 pursue

Exercises 2 and 3 page 115
Answers will vary. Possible answers:
a, c, e

Exercise 4 page 115
Answers will vary. Possible answers:

yes	no
Study of British writers and painters also found high % of mood disorders.	Those artists who do suffer mental illness are more successful when their condition is controlled.
Larger study suggested genetic basis.	Connection is practical not causal.
Similar unusual behavior found in both populations.	

Exercises 5 and 6 page 117
Answers will vary.

Exercise 7 page 118
Answers will vary.

READING 2

Exercise 1 page 118
Answers will vary. (See page 131 in Student's Book for best answer.)

Exercise 2 page 119
1 c
2 a
3 c
4 a
5 b
6 a
7 a
8 c

Exercise 3 page 121
1 M
2 D
3 D
4 M
5 X
6 D
7 M
8 D

Exercise 4 page 122
Answers will vary. Possible answers:
1 breakthroughs that change a field
2 small c
3 everyday problem solving
4 convergent thinking
5 divergent thinking
6 finding a single, best solution
7 generating many possible solutions

Exercise 5 page 122
Answers will vary. Possible answers:
1 Jack Dorsey showed he was good at making associations and connections when he linked texting to sending out taxis.
2 When people procrastinate, they put off doing things until the last minute. This allows ideas to incubate.
3 People with ADHD are easily stimulated and tend to seek novelty, take risks, and push limits. These are things that are important and exciting in hunting but risky and unpredictable.

Exercise 6 page 122
Answers will vary.

LANGUAGE DEVELOPMENT

Exercise page 123
1 conducted the study
2 intervention
3 implications
4 control group
5 experimental group
6 research subjects
7 establish a causal link
8 contend

CRITICAL THINKING

Exercise 1 page 124
Answers will vary.

Exercise 2 page 125
a Reading 1
b Reading 2
c Reading 1, Reading 2
d Reading 1, Reading 2
e Reading 1, Reading 2
f Reading 2
Remaining answers will vary.

Exercise 3 page 125
Answers will vary.

GRAMMAR FOR WRITING

Exercise 1 page 126
1 The articles describe what activities the research subjects did in order to demonstrate their creativity.
2 What has long been considered signs of mental illness may actually be part of the creative process.
3 We still don't know for certain what leads to creativity.
4 The researchers were looking for what singles out the most creative people in the population.
5 Finding what activities creative people are doing when they come up with their best ideas was one of the goals of the study.

Exercise 2 page 127
Answers will vary.

ACADEMIC WRITING SKILLS

Exercise 1 pages 127
1 Kari Stefansson (Reading 1)
   Year: 2015   Source: *The Guardian*
   In a 2015 interview published in *The Guardian*, Kari Stefansson stated, "Often, when people are creating something new, they end up straddling . . . sanity and insanity."
2 Nancy Andreasen (Reading 2)
   Year: 2014   Source: *Atlantic Magazine*
   Nancy Andreasen in an article published in *Atlantic*

Magazine in 2014 explains that creative people are "better at recognizing relationships, making associations and connections, and seeing things in an original way—seeing things that others cannot see."

Exercises 2–5 page 128
Answers will vary.

Exercise 6 page 129
Answers will vary.

ON CAMPUS

Exercise 1 page 132
Answers will vary.

Exercise 2 page 132
1 F
2 T
3 F
4 T
5 T
6 T

Exercise 3 page 132
Answers will vary.

Exercise 4 page 133
Answers will vary.

UNIT 6
ACTIVATE YOUR KNOWLEDGE

page 135
Answers will vary.

WATCH AND LISTEN

Exercises 1 and 2 page 136
Answers will vary.

Exercise 3 page 137
1, 3, 5

Exercise 4 page 137
Answers will vary. Possible answers:
1 4,000 are skilled.
2 He hires 550 workers a year, 360 of which are technical. Some positions remain open for one year.
3 It has been cut by $140 million and may be cut by another 20%.
4 electronics, instrument technical, mechanics

Exercises 5 and 6 page 137
Answers will vary.

READING 1

Exercise 1 page 138
Answers will vary.

Exercise 2 page 138

	figure 1	**figure 2**
horizontal axis	Time: 2006–2015	Time: 2011–2020
vertical axis	percentage of companies who had difficulty filling positions	raw number (number of jobs and qualified graduates)
whole graph	Since 2006, between 30% and 40% of companies have had trouble filling positions.	Since 2011, the number of computing jobs has grown faster than the number of graduates in that field.

Exercise 3 page 139
Answers will vary. Possible answers:
1 There are not enough people able to do the kind of work that companies currently need done.
2 There are not enough students learning the skills necessary to fill the increasing number of jobs that companies will have open.
3 Companies will continue to have large percentages of their positions unfilled if students are not taught the skills needed to do the jobs.

Exercise 4 page 139
1 expertise
2 qualified
3 survey
4 boasts
5 assertive
6 alternative
7 prospective
8 persistent

Exercise 5 page 141
a 5
b 2
c 6
d 1
e 4
f 3

Exercise 6 page 141
d

Exercise 7 page 142
1 DNS
2 T
3 F; The positions that companies are trying to fill often do not require a college education.
4 T
5 F; Education programs have not adapted enough to meet the new demand for technical skills.
6 T
7 DNS
8 F; An unfilled position that remains open for more than three months can cost a company more than $14,000.

Exercise 8 page 142
1 c
2 a

Exercise 9 page 142
Answers will vary.

READING 2

Exercise 1 page 143
Answers will vary. Possible answers:
1 The percentage of people with a college education has increased globally from 2000 to 2012.
2 Median income is the amount of money that divides the top half of a country's earners from the lower half. College graduates are more likely to earn above the median income.
3 The topic of the article will be about the relationship between a college education and income. The argument will likely be that a college education will improve your income.

Exercise 2 page 143
a dispute
b ambiguity
c founders
d diminish
e chronic
f extend
g potential
h illustration

Exercise 3 page 144
1 T
2 F; College graduates in the U.S. make about $17,000 more per year than those with just a high school degree.
3 T
4 DNS
5 F; Liberal arts graduates have lower incomes than graduates with an engineering degree.
6 T

Exercise 4 page 144
1

Exercise 5 page 144

Figure 1:
1 Canada
2 South Korea
3 18

Figure 2:
1 Chile
2 Greece
3 65

Exercises 6 and 7 page 146
Answers will vary.

LANGUAGE DEVELOPMENT

Exercise 1 page 147
1 training program
2 earning power
3 placement rate
4 job market
5 labor force
6 entry level
7 work-life balance

Exercise 2 page 147
a 3 information technology professional
b 2 training program graduate
c 4 labor force participation rate
d 5 college enrollment trends
e 1 median household income

CRITICAL THINKING

Exercises 1–3 pages 148–149
Answers will vary.

GRAMMAR FOR WRITING

Exercise 1 pages 150–151
1 B
2 A
3 D
4 C

Exercise 2 page 151
1 C
2 B
3 D
4 A

Exercise 3 page 151
Answers will vary.

ACADEMIC WRITING SKILLS

Exercise 1 page 152
b

Exercise 2 page 152
Answers will vary.

WRITING TASK

Exercise 1 page 153
Answers will vary. Possible answers:

	Reading 1	**Reading 2**
main point	Employers cannot find enough qualified workers.	A college education is a good investment.
introduction	Two types of jobs in demand: STEM, skilled trades	More people going to college.
section 1	Jobs change quickly Ed. not always match for job market	College Ed: • more likely to work • higher income • healthier • higher job satisfaction
section 2	Businesses—help prepare workers New Ed programs—bridge the gap	• Tech. income > than liberal arts • Liberal arts students have some advs—different way of thinking • higher job satisfaction?

ON CAMPUS

Exercise 1 page 156
Answers will vary.

Exercise 2 page 156

	Daniel	**Hiroko**
Primary	a letters from soldiers	e new data on Zika virus vaccines
Secondary	f a scholarly book about women in the Civil War	d an analysis of a study on hand washing
Tertiary	c a list of soldiers killed in battle	b an encyclopedia article on good bacteria

Exercise 3 page 156
Answers will vary.
Similar: Use primary, secondary, and tertiary sources.
Different: Daniel's primary sources are not from researchers; Hiroko's are.

Exercise 4 page 156

1 primary
2 secondary
3 secondary
4 tertiary
5 secondary
6 tertiary
7 primary
8 primary

Exercise 5 page 157
Answers will vary.

UNIT 7
ACTIVATE YOUR KNOWLEDGE

page 159
Answers will vary.

WATCH AND LISTEN

Exercises 1 and 2 page 160
Answers will vary.

Exercise 3 page 161
1 T
2 F; Superbugs carry genes that are resistant to current antibiotics.
3 T
4 F; Pharmaceutical companies cannot develop new drugs in a short time; it takes over 10 years.

Exercise 4 page 161
1 worked out 4 hours a day. / was a picture of health.
2 simple infections.
3 more than 60% of antibiotics prescribed are unnecessary.
4 people take every day for chronic conditions.

Exercises 5 and 6 page 161
Answers will vary.

READING 1

Exercise 1 page 162
Answers will vary.

Exercise 2 pages 162–163
1 b
2 a
3 a
4 c
5 c
6 c
7 a
8 b

Exercise 3 page 163
c

Exercise 4 page 163
compare and/or contrast two or more things

Exercise 5 page 165
2 full course of meds not taken
3 nontherapeutic use of antibiotics on livestock
5 bacteria develop resistance to antibiotics

Exercise 6 page 165
1 b
2 e
3 a
4 c
5 d

Exercises 7 and 8 page 165
Answers will vary.

READING 2

Exercise 1 page 166
1 a mosquito found in Africa and Asia
2 carries the pathogen chikungunya
3 shows the spread of *Aedes aegypti* and *Aedes albopictus* in the United States
4 The U.S. habitats of the *Aedes aegypti* and *Aedes albopictus* are similar in that both can be found in the southern part of the country. The habitat of the *Aedes albopictus,* however, extends farther north.
5 *Answers will vary.*

Exercise 2 page 166
a detection
b proximity
c surge
d facilitate
e transmission
f confine
g domesticated
h eradicate

Exercise 3 page 168
a

Exercise 4 page 168
a b d f
1 urbanization
2 rainwater sitting in open containers
3 deforestation
4 close proximity to both wild and domesticated animals

Exercise 5 pages 168–169
Chain 1: urbanization
(a) overcrowded cities
(b) no public water sources
(c) mosquitoes breed freely
(d) people collect water
(e) diseases spread more easily

Chain 2: urbanization
(a) habitat destruction
(b) animals and humans live close together
(c) disease is transmitted across species

Exercise 6 page 169
1 *Answers will vary.*
2 (b) new host *Aedes albopictus*
   (c) global warming

Exercise 7 page 169
Answers will vary.

LANGUAGE DEVELOPMENT

Exercise 1 pages 170–171
Answers will vary. Possible answers:
1 promote / facilitate / etc.
2 contributes to / influences / etc.
3 allows / permits
4 triggers / leads to
5 leaving / allowing / etc.

Exercise 2 page 171
Answers will vary.

Exercise 3 page 171
1 access
2 accessible
3 bacterial
4 infection
5 infect
6 mutation
7 prevent
8 preventable
9 preventative
10 resistance
11 resist
12 therapeutic
13 transmit
14 transmittable
15 transmissible
16 viral

Exercise 4 page 171
1 bacterial
2 viral
3 transmitted
4 mutate
5 resistant
6 therapeutic
7 prevent
8 infecting

GRAMMAR FOR WRITING

Exercises 1 and 2 page 175
Answers will vary.

ACADEMIC WRITING SKILLS

Exercise 1 page 176
a causes
b effects

Exercises 2–6 pages 176–177
Answers will vary.

ON CAMPUS

Exercise 1 page 180
Answers will vary.

Exercise 2 page 180
1 B 2 B 3 G 4 G 5 G 6 G

Exercise 3 page 180
2, 3, 5

Exercise 4 page 181
Answers will vary.

UNIT 8
ACTIVATE YOUR KNOWLEDGE

page 183
Answers will vary.

WATCH AND LISTEN

Exercises 1 and 2 page 184
Answers will vary.

Exercise 3 page 185
1 b
2 c
3 a

Exercise 4 page 185
Answers will vary. Possible answers:
1 gather and talk about meetings, go over client reviews
   and have lunch
2 different projects, different workstreams
3 basketball games / one-upmanship
4 humanize / change the tone

Exercises 5 and 6 page 185
Answers will vary.

READING 1

Exercise 1 page 186
Answers will vary.

Exercise 2 page 186
1 enhance
2 coordinate
3 declined
4 accomplished
5 phenomenon
6 differentiate
7 detract from
8 isolate

Exercise 3 page 187
Answers will vary. Possible answers:
1 *Much of the work in today's world is accomplished in teams: in business, in scientific research, in government, on movie sets, and of course, in sports.*
2 *Animal scientist William Muir wondered if he could build such an A-team—with chickens.*
3 *Of course, chickens are not a team, but this kind of group interaction and its effect on production piqued the interest of researchers who study teams and teamwork.*
4 *In looking for an explanation for the different results for different sports, the researchers isolated one important factor—the extent to which a good performance by a team requires its members to coordinate their actions.*
5 *Assembling the ideal team—for sports, business, science, or entertainment—is more complicated than simply hiring the best talent.*

Exercise 4 page 187
1 detract
2 performance
3 basketball
4 coordinate
5 pursue

Exercise 5 page 187
Answers may vary. Possible answers:
a: the extent to which a good performance by a team requires its members to coordinate their actions
b: when there is a lot of talent on a team, some players may begin to make less effort

Exercise 6 page 189
Answers may vary. Possible answers:
1 A-team refers to the best possible team or group of people you could have working together. It is not limited to sports.
2 Pecking order could relate to the fact that some members of the team are better than others and, therefore, have more power in the group.

3 There are two teams on either side of a rope. Both teams tug, or pull, on the rope with the goal of pulling the other team over a line. The team that pulls the hardest wins. The term could be used in other contexts when trying to explain how two groups or teams are fighting over the same thing.

Exercise 7 page 190
Answers will vary.

READING 2

Exercise 1 page 190
Answers will vary.

Exercise 2 page 190
1 F   2 F   3 T   4 T   5 F   6 F

Exercise 3 page 191
a fundamental
b exclusively
c underlie
d gesture
e distraction
f consistent
g apparently
h display

Exercise 4 page 191
Answers will vary. Possible answers:
1 *For years, psychologists have known how to measure the intelligence of individuals, but only recently have they begun to investigate the issue of group intelligence.*
2 *Researchers at Google and MIT have both tackled this question and they believe they finally have a handle on what makes some teams successful.*
3 *Among the finds, the most consistent and significant is that, in effective groups, members spoke for a roughly equal amount of time—not at every meeting or interaction, but across the course of a project.*
4 *The second consistent finding was that members displayed empathy, an understanding of how it might feel to walk in someone else's shoes.*
5 *There were additional findings that support these general ones.*
6 *Understanding group intelligence can help business and other organizations make fundamental changes necessary to improve group performance.*

Exercise 5 page 191
Answers will vary.

Exercise 6 page 193
2 high empathy measures
3 face each other
5 networks include multiple directs of communication
6 more face-to-face meetings

Exercise 7 page 193

Answers will vary. Possible answers:

a: the phenomenon in which the intelligence of a group of people is greater or lesser than the general intelligence of the individuals in the group.

b: a situation in which a person feels comfortable voicing their ideas and believe others with respect and value their input.

Exercise 8 page 193

Answers will vary. Possible answers:

1 have a basic understanding of
2 understand how another person feels and why s/he feels that way
3 so obvious that you don't need to say it

Exercise 9 page 194

Answers will vary.

LANGUAGE DEVELOPMENT

Exercise 1 page 195

Answers will vary. Possible answers:

1 Human error is often the cause of traffic fatalities.
2 There is evidence that lack of sleep leads to both emotional and physical problems.
3 If you know your personality type, you could find the job that is best for you.
4 Typically, tall people make the best basketball players.
5 Generally, people who are obese will develop diabetes.
6 It is widely believed that we will run out of fossil fuels in about 100 years.

Exercise 2 page 195

Answers will vary.

CRITICAL THINKING

Exercise 1 page 196

Answers will vary.

Exercise 2 page 198

organization	goal(s)	challenges
Rockethedge	finding employees to launch a new division	The demands on employees are very high. For example, employees must work long hours and they must always maintain high billing levels
Saxton, CA	to field a professional soccer team in nine months	The city has a limited budget and a short time frame to reach its goal.

organization	goal(s)	challenges
Cybergogo	to get a contract for a big job with a major international food service company	The company has difficulties with completing proposals on time.
Smythe U	to rebuild its track team so the university can increase its fundraising	The university is having difficulty raising money because the track team is performing poorly.

Exercises 3 and 4 page 198

Answers will vary.

GRAMMAR FOR WRITING

Exercises 1 and 2 page 199

Answers will vary.

ACADEMIC WRITING SKILLS

Exercises 1 and 2 page 200

Answers will vary.

ON CAMPUS

Exercise 1 page 204

Answers will vary.

Exercise 2 page 204

1 F
2 DNS
3 T
4 F
5 DNS
6 T
7 T

Exercise 3 page 204

Answers will vary.

Exercise 4 page 205

Answers will vary.

UNIT 1

Reporter: The CD is now a collector's item, replaced by digital downloads. But those who built up music libraries in the 80s and 90s may wonder, how long will those discs work—something Fenella France and her team are hoping to figure out.

Fenella France: You can see this one, it looks pretty good.

Reporter: Right.

France: And then this one.

Reporter: Oh my! France is the chief of preservation research and testing at the Library of Congress.

France: So we've kind of lost the entire reflective layer off of this one.

Reporter: Same CD?

France: Same CD.

Reporter: Produced at the same time.

Reporter: She and her colleagues are studying CDs like this one so they can better understand how to keep them safe for posterity. It turns out not all of the biggest challenges in preserving history involve documents that are centuries old.

One would think, oh, I need to worry about the parchment or the paper degrading, not the things from 20 years ago.

France: That's correct, and that's a challenge, I think. We've always focused on traditional materials, so to speak.

Reporter: How long a CD will last is not as simple as how old it is. Different manufacturers use different methods with vastly different results when it comes to durability.

France: We'd love to be able to say: these particular discs or this specific time, these are the absolute ones at risk. We don't know how people have stored or used them over time, so all of those factors—the use, the handling, the environment—all come into play in terms of the longevity.

Reporter: Which is where the idea of accelerated aging comes in. The CDs are actually cooked in these chambers, and by manipulating the humidity and the temperature, the discs can be aged a certain number of years.

The only thing that's different is how you've artificially aged them?

France: They were aged under the same conditions. One survived, one did not. So that's the challenge we have, that you never quite know how it's going to affect your CD.

Reporter: And if you want to preserve your CD collection at home, here's a few tips.

France: Probably don't put any nice fancy labels onto the top of CDs.

Reporter: And fair warning, you want to avoid those Sharpies.

France: There are some pens that they say don't cause any damage. There's a little piece in the center of the disc, and if you need to, just write on that center region.

Reporter: As for preserving the library's collection, France and her team plan to test the CDs every three to five years to make sure as little as possible is lost to history.

UNIT 2

Man: So, this is what I'm talking about. This is, uh, *Life* magazine, 1953. One ad after another in here—it just kind of shows every single visual bad habit that was, like, endemic in those days. You've got, uh, you know, zany hand lettering everywhere, this swash typography to kind of signify elegance. Exclamation points, exclamation points, exclamation points! Cursive wedding invitation typography down here reading, "Almost everyone appreciates the best." Uh, this was everywhere in the 50s. This is how everything looked in the 50s. You cut to, um—this is after Helvetica was in full swing, same product. No people, no smiling fakery. Just a beautiful, big glass of ice-cold Coke. The slogan underneath: "It's the real thing. Period. Coke. Period." In Helvetica. Period. Any questions? Of course not. Drink Coke. Period. Simple.

Leslie Savan: Governments and corporations love Helvetica because, on one hand, it makes them seem neutral and efficient; but also, it's the smoothness of the letters, makes them seem almost human. That is a quality they all want to convey because, of course, they have the image they're always fighting, that they are authoritarian, they're bureaucratic, you lose yourself in them, they're oppressive. So instead, by using Helvetica, they can come off seeming more accessible, transparent, and accountable.

UNIT 3

Gayle King (co-host): Now to the photo hacking scandal everybody's talking about. As we told you earlier, Apple now says those nude celebrity images were stolen in, quote, "... a very targeted attack on user names, passwords, and security questions ...", adding that "None of the cases we have investigated has resulted from a breach in any of Apple's systems including iCloud® or Find my iPhone." The FBI is now on the case, so we wanted to look at the bigger implications of this. CBS news legal analyst Rikki Klieman joins us from Boston. Rikki, good morning to you.

Rikki Klieman: Good morning.

King: Hey, how is the FBI involved in the case? What exactly are they doing?

Klieman: Well, the FBI is going to look at all of the systems. Despite Apple saying that it really comes from the idea of "forgot your password," they will be looking at the devices belonging to these movie stars—that is, their mobile phones, their computers, their backup systems—and they will also then be searching to look for, in essence, the virtual fingerprints of the hackers themselves.

King: So who do you think could be charged here, the hackers, the websites? The people that posted the videos, the pictures?

Klieman: Well, you have to look from the greatest to the smallest. We know that the hackers can be charged. There's a law on the books as far back as 1986, and it's called the Computer Fraud and Abuse Act. And that's really the big law, because what we have there are penalties for each count, each hacking, and that goes to five years a count and even, with enhancements, it may be more than that. You may remember that there was a case where Scarlett Johansson among others, her nude photos were hacked. The person in Florida who did that, a man by the name of Christopher Chaney, he wound up with a 10-year plea on the basis of nine counts. So he could have gotten a lot more than that. What we look at after that is people who have put it on the website—it's the people who put it up there that may become liable, both criminally and civilly. The website's not going to be liable, and certainly the people who look at it are not going to be liable.

Norah O'Donnell (co-host): Can I ask you about—there are certainly a lot of headlines out there where people are saying, you know, this isn't just a scandal, it's a sex crime against these women.

Klieman: Well, it's not a sex crime against these women. Uh, the reality of this is, it is a computer crime and a computer crime only, despite the fact that it's this kind of public exposure of something that is really private. When we have something in our cell phone, we have a reasonable expectation of privacy, that no one is going to look at that. But it doesn't mean that by someone hacking into it and putting it out there that it is a sex crime. In fact, the worst part of all of this is—if I read one more thing about people blaming the victims in this case. If you take a photo in the privacy of your own home, with your husband, with

your significant other, or all by yourself—and then let alone the fact that some of these photos were deleted—why, in heaven's name, do you expect that some hacker is going to go in there? That is not, it just is not a reasonable expectation of privacy. It is your own, and we shouldn't blame the victim.

Charlie Rose (co-host): Thank you so much, Rikki.

UNIT 4

Anna Werner (reporter): Willow Tufano may look like a typical teen, dress like one, and act like one, but growing up during Florida's foreclosure crisis gave her the opportunity to become something else, too.

Willow Tufano: I bought my first house and I'm buying my second house here soon.

Werner: You're a landlord?

Tufano: Yes.

Werner: She's likely Florida's youngest landlord, taking her cues from her realtor mom who buys cheap, bank-owned homes.

Tufano: I would go around with my mom and look at these houses, and there was one that was filled with a whole bunch of furniture that was nice, and I said, well, I could sell this stuff. So that was how it started.

Werner: Willow eventually made $6,000 by selling furniture, which she used to help her purchase this $12,000 home. She'll soon close on her second house, this one. It costs $17,500.

Tufano: I'm trying to get as many houses as I can while the market is low.

Werner: What's your goal?

Tufano: I want to have probably around 10 houses by the time that I'm 18.

Werner: 10?

Tufano: Yes, I want to try for two a year, pretty much.

Werner: Today, Willow spends her spare time gathering and selling items not just from foreclosed homes but from garage sales, from charities, even street curbs.

Tufano: I just try and save every penny that I can to invest in more houses.

Werner: As a minor, Willow can't legally be on the deed. But when she turns 18, her mother, Shannon Moore, will sign the properties over to her.

Shannon Moore: I said, "Willow, lead the way. Show me where you need to go." And she has.

Werner: Not bad for a kid with attention deficit hyperactivity disorder who left a gifted school because teachers told her mom her daughter couldn't focus.

Moore: I guess it's hard to, you know, listen to people say your kid has a problem, you know. And then now look at her. I don't know, I guess I'm really proud of her.

Werner: These days Willow's busy collecting rent from her tenants, shopping for building materials, and taking stock of her next project.

Moore: I think that would work.

Werner: All from a girl who is too young to drive but has plenty of direction. Anna Werner, CBS News, North Port, Florida.

UNIT 5

Charlie Rose (co-host): For 30 years David Kelley and his brother Tom have taken familiar products and made them better. Their design firm IDEO reengineered everything from the computer mouse to television remote controls and even the classroom chair. Now the brothers have put out a new book. It is called *Creative Confidence: Unleashing the Creative Potential within All of Us* [sic]. David and Tom Kelley, welcome.

David and Tom Kelley: Thanks.

Rose: So what is creative confidence?

Tom Kelley: Well, it's really two things. It's the natural human ability to come up with breakthrough ideas combined with the courage to act on those ideas. Because, when we did a hundred interviews for the book, what we discovered is some people have the ideas but they—they have fear of being judged, and so they just hold it all in, and then their idea disappears. And so it's the—it's the ability to come up with the ideas but the courage, too.

Gayle King (co-host): And you both believe that everybody can be creative. I tell you, after looking at the book, I am thinking differently. You said *everybody*. I've never believed that.

David Kelley: Yeah, well, look at little kids in kindergarten.

King: Yes.

David Kelley: Everybody, you know, they're like, they're making like, uh, you know, a picture of a chicken with four legs, and mom puts it up on the refrigerator and says, "Yay!" So, we all have it in kindergarten, and somewhere along the line—

King: In fourth grade, you say.

David Kelley: Yeah, I think it's about fourth grade, you opt out and think of yourself as not creative because you're kind of being judged by your peers, or a teacher tells you that's not a very good drawing, or whatever. And it's just—it's just too bad.

Norah O'Donnell (co-host): I have young children and, you know, I see this happen early on in schools. They say, "Oh, that child is very creative," you know? And you get the assumption that people are born creative, and yet you do not believe that, as Gayle mentioned earlier. But you also think you can teach and continue to foster creativity.

David Kelley: Yeah, I mean, it's funny, you know. Somehow we have, sort of, *creativity* tied up with, kind of, *talent*, and it's really not the case. So, you know, you don't really expect a person to sit down at the piano and play for the first time. You know, like, that would be crazy. But we somehow think that either you can draw or you can't draw. You know, like, some—drawing takes just as much practice as playing the piano does and so, um, you find your different ways. You may be a creative curator. You may be a creative person who, you know, figures things out in new ways and still can't draw. Right? But, so, creativity is—needs to be defined as the ability to, kind of, come up with new ideas in, kind of, unique ways. If you think about being creative, if you just take all the little parts of a project, what that adds to—and then you say, how can I make this little piece, you know, extraordinary? How can I make this little piece extraordinary?

King: For someone who is listening to you, what is the first thing we should do if we think, I'm not creative.

David Kelley: Yeah.

King: I want to be creative.

David Kelley: Yeah, so, get the book.

King: Other than that.

David Kelley: But the whole thing is—is getting in and building empathy for people. We find that—we see this thing called "bias towards action" where you jump right in. I mean, so many people spend time planning and think, I'm going to go. Instead, just jump in. If you're designing a new, you know, uh, bicycle, go out and watch people ride bicycles. Talk to people who don't ride bicycles. Ride a bicycle yourself. Go to the stores. I mean, all of that, we call it empathy. You're having empathy for the people. If I'm trying to please a certain person, I really want to build empathy for them. And I think it's, kind of, an underserved area. We mostly look at technology or business.

Rose: Yes.

David Kelley: And come up with those kind of ideas and then try to convince people to—that they might like it. It's much better, I believe, to go out and, like, really build empathy for people. What do they really want? What's meaningful to people is really where we go. If it's meaningful for people, then in some ways it's easier to go find technologies and business ideas that solve that particular problem.

UNIT 6

Nick Sinetti: I don't really dig the second shift, but you've got to start somewhere.

Reporter: Despite the worst job market in decades, listen to what 20-year-old Nick Sinetti found right out of high school.

How many offers did you get?

Sinetti: Um, three, I think.

Reporter: Three offers?

Sinetti: Right.

Reporter: He graduated in 2009 as a certified welder from a career in technical education high school, or what used to be called vocational education. He now works for Air Products in Allentown, Pennsylvania.

Of the 7,500 employees that you have here in the United States, how many are, what you would say, are the skilled workers?

John McGlade: 4,000.

Reporter: John McGlade is president and CEO of Air Products. His global company designs and builds high-tech hydrogen equipment and devices.

How worried are you that you won't find enough skilled workers in the future?

McGlade: I'm worried. I've been worried.

Reporter: McGlade says he hires about 550 U.S. workers a year—360 are technically skilled positions that require two years of college or advanced certification. These positions can often go unfilled for twelve months.

McGlade: You need people who are electronics experts, who are instrument technicians, who are mechanics that can work on today's modern equipment.

Reporter: But this year funding for vocational education was cut by $140 million, and President Obama is proposing a 20% cut next year.

What is your, sort of, biggest fear if there isn't this continued support for vo-tech education?

McGlade: Without the support and without the continued development of the skilled workforce, um, we're not going to be able to fill the jobs.

Reporter: Lehigh Career and Technical Institute would be impacted as well. Five percent of its budget comes from federal grants.

Teacher: 24 divided by 1.5E, that tells us—

Reporter: The school trains about 3,000 students from across the Lehigh Valley. According to the National Association of Career and Technical schools, these students can earn about $26 an hour more than similar students in non-technical fields.

McGlade: There's going to be more and more of those skilled jobs available that are going to be well paying and be a sustainable career for years and years to come.

Reporter: A career path that McGlade estimates will need 10 million more skilled workers over the next decade.

UNIT 7

Tom Dukes: I never thought it would happen to me.

Katie Couric (reporter): Tom Dukes was the picture of health, an energetic 52-year-old sales executive in Lomita, California, who worked out four hours a day until late last year when he was rushed to the hospital in agonizing pain. An hour later he was on the operating table.

Dukes: I thought, you know, I might just be saying goodbye. That was my last thought.

Couric: Dukes awoke to a shocking reality. Surgeons had to repair a hole in his abdomen caused by a raging E. coli infection developed after eating contaminated meat. This form of E. coli was much more aggressive because it had several genetic mutations making it resistant to antibiotics.

Dukes: Everything was getting, you know, progressively worse quickly.

Couric: Duke's story concerns infectious disease doctors, like Brad Spellberg, author of *Rising Plague*.

Brad Spellberg: These organisms are the experts at resistance.

Couric: He says more infections are starting out as bacteria in food or other ordinary places and evolving into deadly, drug-resistant superbugs.

Spellberg: It is starting to move out of the hospitals and into the communities.

Couric: And what happens to those people?

Spellberg: We're at a point where we may have to start admitting tens of thousands of women with simple urinary tract infections to the hospital.

Couric: Because that infection has outsmarted the pills?

Spellberg: Yep. Because the E. coli that causes most urinary tract infections is becoming resistant.

Couric: Health officials say that resistance is growing, especially among these five deadly bacteria. Virtually all of them carry genes that prevent antibiotics from working, and these genetic mutations are spreading. Another reason for these lethal strains—the overuse of antibiotics. A recent study finds more than 60% of antibiotics prescribed are unnecessary.

John Rex: It's a crisis that touches every country on the globe, touches people of all socioeconomic classes, all races.

Chemist: This represents the compounds that we're making—

Couric: John Rex is the head of drug development for AstraZeneca—one of only a few pharmaceutical companies still devoting resources for new medicines to cure these lethal bugs.

Rex: The trick is to find something that kills the bacteria but doesn't hurt you or me.

Couric: Developing a new antibiotic takes at least ten years and costs as much $1.7 billion. Drug companies make more money creating medicines people take every day for chronic conditions like high blood pressure, insomnia, or sexual dysfunction.

Do you consider this a grave public health crisis?

Spellberg: Yeah. This is a convergence of two public health crises: skyrocketing antibiotic resistance and dying antibiotic development.

Dukes: I was extremely fatigued. I was mentally exhausted.

Couric: It took four months and several drugs for Tom Dukes to finally beat his infection, but he says he'll never completely recover.

Dukes: I think about it every day because if it hadn't worked, I wouldn't be here.

UNIT 8

Carisa Bianci: The company is an advertising agency, but we like to think of ourselves as a creative company. So I think the space was designed to just allow creative thoughts and thinking.

Carol Madonna: Our architect was really smart. He provided us with really indelible materials. We have a thousand 27-year-olds here. They are pretty hard on stuff.

Jayanta Jenkins: The space in itself is designed for collaboration, so I think the mindset just, kind of, you know, very, sort of, fluidly flows that way here.

Jason Clement: I think we really have created this, uh, sense of a city in here where you really have what you need. You know, places where we congregate. We have places where we go away. There are communities, so we're organized by, you know, different projects and different work streams. So, you know, you get a sense of going from, you know, one part of town to another part of town.

Bianci: Main Street is where the creatives are, so all the square boxes there and the three layers of that, that's, kind of, Main Street.

Clement: You can get to the other side of the building by really walking across almost like a catwalk.

Jenkins: The part where we're sitting is a communal space where people can gather to talk about meetings, to go over client reviews, to have lunch.

William Esparza: When it comes to work, it just eliminates the seriousness, you know, and so you can start having ideas and have synergy happen between people informally.

Clement: But you can get work done without having to feel this formality, right, of needing to schedule time or needing to schedule a place to be able to get it done.

Bianci: People can pull over 100 hours a week. Um, it's—it's not uncommon. If you're in a new business pitch, you do a lot of all-nighters. You'll come here on the weekends and there's quite a few cars in the parking lot. You come back the next day, and they're wearing the same outfit that they have. So I think there're spaces here that people can, kind of, crash. Um, there's a whole dog community here.

Clement: Dogs add a lot to a meeting, right, in terms of just humanizing it. I think we can have really tough meetings. We can disagree on things, and if a meeting is particularly tough and somebody starts licking your ankle, it really changes your tone.

Bianci: We tend to do basketball games as well. After hours you're going to see people running up and down that court.

Clement: Everybody shows up and we can get together as a family and share good news and sometimes bad news.

Bianci: I think, you know, whenever someone sees something that they respect and admire, you know, it gives them that, kind of like, all right, you know, I'm going to go and I'm going to, like, take it on, and I want to deliver something as good or better. It's a healthy competitiveness.

Esparza: Whether it's the Gatorade team or the Pepsi team, there's a sense of one-upmanship. You know, you want to make the best work out of the building.

Jenkins: The thing that isn't so nice about an open office plan sometimes is people can always walk in, but if you're really working and don't want to be interrupted, uh, it's nice to find areas in the building where you can see people but they can't see you. You can easily get a lot of work done where people wouldn't be able to find you unless, you know, you decided that you wanted to be found.

Right up above here is this billboard that has one of the Pepsi, um, adverts that we did, and right behind it is the perfect hiding place.

Madonna: We're nurturing everybody and helping them, you know, flourish here, but we also rule with an iron fist.

Name: _____   Date: _____

Read the essay. Then answer the questions that follow.

The Native American Land Conservancy

1   The Native Americans who live in present-day California are the descendants of the indigenous peoples who lived in the area before the arrival of European settlers. According to a recent United States census report, over 300,000 people living in California today have Native American heritage. Despite this, most areas in the state that have cultural and historical significance for Native American tribes are not owned or controlled by tribes. Ongoing plans made by property developers, as well as pollution, threaten to destroy places that have historically been important to native people. Because many Native American communities do not have access to their sacred sites and find it difficult to protect their own traditional cultures, groups like the Native American Land Conservancy (NALC) have been formed. The NALC started in 1998 as an inter-tribal group focused on protecting sacred sites in Southern California. A review of some examples of the work that the NALC does demonstrates the organization's importance and shows why it should have the support of all Americans.

2   In 2004, the NALC collaborated with tribal representatives and conservation groups to acquire and protect an area called Horse Canyon in the Santa Rosa Mountains. This area is part of the Colorado Desert, which contains evidence of the societies of early native peoples. This includes ancient trails, rock shelters, quarry sites, and examples of rock art. In the past, tribes would use the area for ritual hunting activities. If it were not for the support of the NALC, this area might now be a housing development.

3   The Cahuilla Fish Traps Program is another example of the good work that the NALC does. Working with an organization called the Trust for Public Lands, they monitor an ancient Native American site and act as tribal representatives. The Salton Sea is the name of a lake in Southern California where ancient fish traps were carved into the rocks by members of the Cahuilla tribe. This site has long been of cultural and historical importance to the local Native American community. However, because of the extensive use of off-road vehicles, the archeological evidence has been vulnerable to pollution. By monitoring this site, the NALC and other groups can both register and record those who use the area and encourage protective measures. They also maintain an informational facility on the property.

4   Finally, the NALC has been instrumental in conserving the area called Old Woman Mountains Preserve in San Bernardino County. This area surrounds a group of mountains, and it includes a large granite rock that is thought to resemble an old woman. The 2,560-acre preserve contains many places with historical and cultural ties to various Native American tribes. In 2002, the NALC purchased it with the goal of improving hiking trails, protecting the landscape, and running educational programs. They now conduct scientific surveys of the plants and animals found on the property. Especially important is the Learning Landscape program for tribal young people, which teaches them about their own cultural traditions.

5   It is plain to see that the NALC is helping to conserve both the environment and Native American culture with such projects just as the National Park Service preserves Alcatraz Island and Muir Woods for the good of the country. After all, the history of the native people in California is just as important as any other history of the region, and we must support groups like the NALC in their goals. It is abundantly clear that, without the assistance of groups like the NALC, places of cultural and historical importance to Native American tribes in California would not be maintained and conserved. All United States citizens must remember that the legacy of the native tribes and the land they have lived on is part of our shared history.

PART A KEY SKILLS

IDENTIFYING AN ARGUMENT

1 Choose the best answer to each question.

1 What is the writer's main argument?
   a The NALC deserves the support of all Americans due to its proven work of preserving tribal history, culture, and the environment.
   b The NALC works with other organizations to protect important Native American sites.
   c Native Americans need organizations like the NALC to help them conserve their sacred land.

2 Which argument is *not* presented in this essay?
   a Areas of importance to Native Americans should be preserved.
   b Land that is in danger of being polluted should be protected.
   c Developers should be allowed to construct buildings on land that is not sacred to Native Americans.

3 Why does the author mention that *all* Americans should support the NALC?
   a to emphasize that the issue of conserving land, culture, and history is not limited to Native Americans
   b to prove that the NALC has not had the support of many people in the past
   c to argue that tribes in California have been discriminated against and deserve financial compensation

IDENTIFYING SUPPORTING DETAILS

2 Match the paragraphs to the statements.

1 Paragraph 2 _____   a An area containing evidence of historical Native American culture was saved
2 Paragraph 3 _____   from development.
3 Paragraph 4 _____   b An area that is important to Native Americans is now the site of an
                                educational program for young people.
                             c An area of archeological importance was saved from the dangers of pollution.

3 Choose all correct answers.

1 What reasons does the author give for the founding of the NALC?
   a More than 300,000 people now live in endangered areas.
   b Native American lands face threats from property developers.
   c Many Native Americans do not have access to their sacred historical sites.
   d Native Americans have fewer rights than other California residents.

2 Which example(s) does the writer discuss to support his thesis?
   a Cahuilla Fish Traps Program
   b Old Woman Mountains Preserve
   c Horse Canyon
   d Muir Woods

3 Which detail(s) about the NALC does the author include?
   a The NALC sponsors hunting trips.
   b The NALC monitors recreational use.
   c The NALC carries out scientific surveys.
   d The NALC takes legal action against land developers.
   e The NALC builds trails and rock shelters.
   f The NALC provides educational resources.

4 Which idea is mentioned in the conclusion but not the introduction?
   a Conservation of certain land areas is important, and many people are not aware of this.
   b Native American heritage is something that all U.S. citizens share as a community.
   c The history of Native Americans in the state of California is especially important.

PART B ADDITIONAL SKILLS

4 Choose the best answer to each question.

1 Which statement do you think the author would agree with most?
   a Preservation of Native American history and culture is the most important function of the NALC.
   b Protection of the natural environment in Southern California is the most important contribution of the NALC.
   c The NALC's work preserving Native American history and culture, and protecting the environment are equally important.

2 In paragraph 2, why does the author mention "ritual hunting activities"?
   a He is against the hunting of animals.
   b He thinks that knowing this information can help us understand more about past cultures.
   c He wants to emphasize that Native Americans hunted based on specific rules.

3 What was the author's main purpose for writing this essay?
   a to educate the reader about an organization he admires
   b to criticize the government of California and offer solutions
   c to describe some different Native American tribes of Southern California

4 How would you describe the overall tone of this essay?
   a sarcastic
   b informative
   c disappointed

5 How does the author end the essay?
   a with a warning
   b with a prediction
   c with a call to action or suggestion

Name: _____ Date: _____

PART A KEY VOCABULARY

1   Complete the paragraphs with the correct form of the words in the box.

> capacity   deliberate   emerge   memorabilia
> practice   prompt   recover   vulnerable

Using sustainable methods for growing crops is an environmentally beneficial
(1)_____ . This has (2)_____ many agriculturalists to study more ways to farm
sustainably. They are also studying ways to grow crops without harming the surrounding
ecology, including fish and other marine life that are (3)_____ to the damaging effects
of contaminated lake water. In many cases, contaminating water is not a (4)_____ act;
farmers may not even know that their practices are harmful. Nevertheless, if there is too much
pollution in a lake, the fish population may never (5)_____ , and could eventually die off.

In recent years, several private organizations have (6)_____ with the goal of
conserving traditional Native American land in North America. In addition, they focus on
maintaining tribal history by collecting historical documents and (7)_____ , and using
them to educate the public through museums and school programs. These groups have the
(8)_____ to make a difference in our society.

2   Complete the notice with the correct form of the words in the box.

> affordable   deteriorate   developer   facility
> maintain   prosper   renovation   vacant

To Whom It May Concern:

A property (1)_____ in our town has identified buildings that are currently
(2)_____ – in other words, not being lived in. Several of these buildings in the garden
district of our town are in bad condition and are (3)_____ quickly. She (4)_____
that her company would be able to make the buildings livable again through a series of
(5)_____ . Her plan is to create new homes with community (6)_____ , such as
playgrounds and running trails. She is requesting financial support from our office so that these
homes could serve as (7)_____ housing for families with low incomes. Having decent
homes will help all members of our community (8)_____ , not just the middle and
upper classes.

Sincerely,
The Office of Community Development

PART B LANGUAGE DEVELOPMENT
TIME EXPRESSIONS

3 Complete the sentences with the correct expressions in the box.

> at one time   at the turn of the century
> for the time being   out of date   slowly but surely

1 In 1900, there were approximately 1.65 billion people on earth. One hundred years later, _____ , there were over 6 billion.
2 The first few times I took my son skating he had trouble even standing on the ice. However, _____ , he learned to skate, and this year he was selected for the local ice hockey team.
3 _____ , many years ago, there was a forest here instead of a town.
4 If the medicine in your cabinet is _____ , you should get rid of it because it may not be safe to use.
5 We would like to buy a new car but cannot afford one right now, so _____ we have to continue using our old one.

COMPOUND ADJECTIVES

4 Choose the correct compound adjectives to complete the sentences.

a Beyoncé is a *well known / well-known* singer of empowering pop music.
b Although he is quite wealthy now, he grew up in a *low income / low-income* family.
c It is often true that *fast growing / fast-growing* countries experience environmental problems.
d I try to stay *up to date / up-to-date* by reading several respectable news sources.
e The project to conserve more state forests is a *long term / long-term* plan that we hope will survive the current administration's budget cuts.

Name: _____   Date: _____

PART A GRAMMAR IN WRITING
FUTURE CONDITIONALS

1 Read the sentences. Circle *R* (real conditional) or *U* (unreal conditional).

1	If the pollution in the lakes were even worse than it is now, all of the fish would die.	R	U
2	If you drive an off-road vehicle near that nature preserve, you will harm the environment.	R	U
3	You will learn more about Native American culture if you visit the Old Woman Mountains.	R	U
4	If we were to allow pollution levels to rise in the Salton Sea, it would be a disaster.	R	U
5	If groups do not continue to receive support, a great deal of California's history will be lost.	R	U

PART B WRITING TASK

> Is environmental conservation more important than land development in your state, region, or country? Give reasons and examples to support your argument.

2 Write an argumentative essay that answers the writing prompt. Include an introductory paragraph with a clear thesis statement, at least two body paragraphs, and a concluding paragraph.

Name: _____ Date: _____

Read the article. Then answer the questions that follow.

A Rebranding Success Story

1   Rebranding a business that has been in the market for a long time is very difficult, but there are some notable examples of companies that have benefited from doing so. One of the most successful efforts in the contemporary business era was launched by Apple Computers. To understand how this happened, we need to go back to the early 1990s. At that time, technology products were mostly targeted to men, not to women or children. Furthermore, appealing advertising and price were considered more important when marketing products to the average buyer than product innovation. Apple Computers was not meeting its sales goals or generating enough consumer interest in its products. Their computer, the Macintosh, was innovative but expensive. There was also a lot of competition to deal with, which made it harder for the company to present itself as unique. In fact, Apple was in danger of going bankrupt.

2   Things changed when Steve Jobs returned to the company to serve as its chief executive officer (CEO). Jobs was a co-founder of the company in the 1970s, but he had left in 1985. He was asked to come back and run Apple in 1997. Jobs had a vision based on the idea of thinking differently, which led to the new Apple slogan "Think Different." Working with Apple technicians, he wanted to create computers that would appeal to a much wider segment of the marketplace. The first product to emerge from this new phase of the company was a new version of the Macintosh called the iMac. The iMac did not look like any personal computers (PCs) that had come before it: it had an egg-shaped design and a playful image. iMacs were also candy colored, which was not something that had previously been associated with computers. Apple worked hard to make a new kind of PC that was easy for consumers to set up and easy to use. Sales took off: people were willing to pay more for these iMacs, and Apple became a dominant force in the market. Apple was no longer just another computer company.

3   But it was not only the new product design that changed the perception of Apple. The "Think Different" advertising campaign featured a memorable television commercial with images of such famous, innovative people throughout history as Gandhi, Martin Luther King, Jr., and Pablo Picasso. Print advertisements and posters also featured the "Think Different" slogan with images of famous innovators. Many people found the ads inspiring, which was the goal of the rebranding campaign.

4   As one expert at entrepreneurs.com remarked, the Apple team devoted its energies to creating a superior and desirable product. In addition to this, they were successful in convincing consumers that they were a great business. They soon successfully expanded the brand to include devices in many different product categories, most notably smartphones and tablets. It was no longer "Apple Computers," but simply "Apple Inc." By 2012, Apple had become the world's most valuable brand.

PART A KEY SKILLS
TAKING NOTES IN OUTLINE FORM

1 Complete the outline with information from the article.

> I. Apple needed to rebrand in 1990s
>
>   A. Mainly men as target market
>
>   B. Advertising & (1) _____ considered more important than
>
>   (2) _____
>
>   C. Lack of success
>
>   1. Not meeting (3) _____
>
>   2. Macintosh: innovative but (4) _____
>
>   3. Lots of (5) _____
>
>   4. Danger of (6) _____
>
> II. Steve Jobs (1997—rejoins company as CEO)
>
>   A. New slogan
>
>   B. New computer: iMac
>
>   1. egg-shaped design
>
>   2. (7) _____
>
>   3. candy-colored
>
>   4. easy to (8) _____ & (9) _____
>
>   C. Sales took off; iMacs were a hit
>
> III. Ad campaign: (10) " _____ _____ "
>
>   A. TV commercial with images of (11) _____ _____
>
>   B. Other types of ads: print, (12) _____
>
> IV. Apple's success
>
>   A. Superior, desirable product
>
>   B. Other products: smartphones, (13) _____
>
>   C. Name change: (14) _____
>
>   D. 2012: world's (15) _____

MAKING INFERENCES

2 Choose the best answer to each question.

1 Why does the author give some details of the PC market in the 1990s?
    a to help readers understand Apple's need to rebrand
    b to explain why Steve Jobs had left Apple
    c to point out that Apple was not the only company selling PCs at that time

2 How did Apple expand their target market?
    a It designed a new logo.
    b It refocused on design and ease of use.
    c It lowered its prices.

3 What does the author imply about other PCs when describing the iMac?
    a They were similar in appearance, but not as colorful.
    b They were more serious and appropriate for certain customers.
    c They were boring and more common by comparison.

4 What can you infer about the "Think Different" campaign as part of Apple's successful rebranding effort?
    a It was one important factor.
    b It was not as important as the innovations of the iMac.
    c It was the most important factor.

5 Why does the author wait until the end of the article to mention Apple's smartphones and tablets?
    a He wants to focus on Apple computers in this article.
    b These products came out after the rebranding had already happened.
    C He assumes his readers are already familiar with these products.

Name: _____   Date: _____

PART A KEY VOCABULARY

1   Complete the sentences with the correct form of the words in the box.

| appropriate   contemporary   criteria   devoted to   opposition to   resemble   resist   subsequent |

1   While Tom is very serious about his career, he is also _____ his family. They are his top priority.
2   The first edition of the history book did not cover the 2000s, but a _____ edition added updated information.
3   The two companies' logos are not exactly the same, but they do _____ each other a bit in shape and color.
4   Wearing a swimming suit at the beach is expected, but it would not be _____ to wear one at the office.
5   Due to strong _____ the plan by environmentalists, the company decided not to build the factory near the river.
6   I usually try to eat in a healthy way, but it is difficult for me to _____ my mother's delicious apple pie with ice cream.
7   Some people like classic or old-style architecture, but I prefer _____ architecture.
8   We can judge a company by several different _____ , including sales information, ethical practices, and service to the community.

2   Complete the sentences with the correct form of the words in the box.

| appeal to   associate   donation   evolve   human rights   modify   opt for   retain |

1   I studied Russian for several years in high school, but I've forgotten most of it. I've only _____ a few words and phrases.
2   Advertisers know that people tend to like songs that they _____ with happy times from their past.
3   What started out as a business school project eventually _____ into a successful company.
4   When I no longer want certain clothes, I give them to nonprofit organizations that accept _____ from the public.
5   According to international law, torture is a violation of our fundamental _____ .
6   At the last minute, the architect had to _____ her design for the new building to conform to a new environmental rule.
7   The advertiser changed the marketing campaign in order to _____ young women, not just middle-aged men.
8   The next time I buy a car, I am going to _____ a model that uses less gasoline than my current one does.

PART B LANGUAGE DEVELOPMENT
DESCRIBING EMOTIONAL RESPONSES

3 Complete the verb-noun collocations in the sentences with appropriate words from the box.

| awe | emotions | outrage | suspicion | trouble |

1 The proposal to replace the children's playground with a new office building has provoked
_____ in our community.
2 My coworkers warned me that if I criticized the boss's plan, it might stir up _____ for all of us.
3 For most visitors, the Grand Canyon inspires _____ due to its size and beauty.
4 The fact that he was in the office alone at 2:00 a.m. has aroused _____ about his
activities there.
5 Seeing the old photographs of my grandparents when they were still alive evoked a whole range of
_____ , from sadness to joy.

PARAPHRASING

4 Paraphrase the sentences. Use synonyms and change the grammatical structure and organization of ideas
without changing the original meaning.

1 Advertisers will probably not win over younger consumers if they create ads that appeal to their parents.

    _____

    _____

    _____

2 A company that wants to rebrand itself needs to do more than just change its logo or slogan, since these
changes will not be enough to change their image.

    _____

    _____

    _____

3 A good way to introduce young adults to new personal care products is to give away samples at colleges.

    _____

    _____

    _____

4 Some companies decide to rebrand because their product sales are decreasing, while others do it in order
to increase the number of customers for already successful products.

    _____

    _____

    _____

5 It is not necessary for logos to be fancy or colorful; some of the most well-known brand logos are
uncomplicated and use one color.

    _____

    _____

    _____

Name: _____   Date: _____

PART A GRAMMAR FOR WRITING
NONIDENTIFYING RELATIVE CLAUSES

1   Rewrite the sentences to include the additional information using relative clauses.

   1   Nike's logo is sometimes called the "swoosh."
     Additional information: The logo is recognized around the world.

     _____
     _____
     _____

   2   More and more companies are emphasizing environmental friendliness in their marketing.
     Additional information: Environmental friendliness is important to consumers.

     _____
     _____
     _____

   3   Marketing a product can be quite expensive.
     Additional information: Marketing a product includes many different ways to get attention for it.

     _____
     _____
     _____

   4   Apple is now considered the most valuable company in the world.
     Additional information: Apple successfully rebranded itself in the 1990s.

     _____
     _____
     _____

   5   The target market for PCs used to be mostly male customers.
     Additional information: The target market now includes practically everyone.

     _____
     _____
     _____

APPOSITIVES

2 Rewrite the sentences to include the additional information using appositives.

1 A slogan can be a key part of a successful marketing campaign.
Additional information: A logo is the phrase a company uses for its marketing.

_____

_____

2 Warby Parker found success by selling inexpensive yet fashionable glasses.
Additional information: Warby Parker is an eyewear retailer.

_____

_____

3 John Pemberton developed the original formula for Coca-Cola in the 19th century.
Additional information: John Pemberton was a pharmacist in Atlanta.

_____

_____

4 SoulCycle has had great success in marketing exercise as fun and friendship instead of work.
Additional information: SoulCycle is a New York-based fitness company

_____

_____

5 The Harry Potter books were originally marketed to children and young adults only.
Additional information: The Harry Potter books are international bestsellers.

_____

_____

_____

PART B WRITING TASK

> Describe and analyze a successful product or packaging design.

3 Choose a design. Write two to three paragraphs in which you describe and analyze
the design and explain why you think it has been successful.

Name: _____   Date: _____

Read the article. Then answer the questions that follow.

Dealing with Digital Identity Theft

1   Now that many transactions in modern life are done digitally, we all have to deal with the possibility of digital identity theft. This problem can take many forms. Of course, there is always the risk of someone stealing and then using your credit card number to purchase something illegally. However, this problem can occur on a larger scale, too. We often hear in the news about certain businesses being hacked; recent examples in the U.S. include the home improvement supply store Home Depot and the technology company Yahoo. As a result, we logically worry that someone may violate the law and access our credit card data. Instances of organizations like health insurance companies being hacked for sensitive medical information are also increasingly in the news. In these cases, companies and organizations may offer the victims of data breaches free identity-theft-protection services to protect against further damage.

2   Identity theft protection after a data breach comes in several forms. The first type is Internet surveillance. Some cybersecurity firms have technology that scans a variety of black market websites, social media platforms, and chatrooms to uncover communications related to illegal selling or trading of stolen personal information. When a firm comes up with evidence that this is happening, it lets the victims know immediately. Other companies provide careful monitoring of bank account information, loan activity, social security number data, credit card activity, and payroll accounts of employers. There are also organizations that can offer support in restoring people's financial reputation after fraud has occurred. A victim's original reputation as an honest customer, business partner, or loan recipient can be harmed indefinitely by identity theft. These firms can help those victims eliminate bad credit scores and clear their names.

3   In addition to the help that firms can provide, there is a lot the individuals themselves can do to guard against identity theft. In a July 2015 article in *The Atlantic* magazine, Costis Toregas, of the Cyber Security Policy and Research Institute at George Washington University, advises victims of data breaches to learn more about strategies to improve their cybersecurity and to make changes in their online practices. He states that, unfortunately, victims of a data breach need to assume that someone has stolen and will attempt to use their personal information at least once, and they need to make online decisions based on this assumption. So what are some of his helpful strategies? One is to review your credit regularly: make sure all purchases listed in your accounts are actually yours. Also, make sure no one is opening new credit accounts in your name. If you do find evidence of fraud, it is recommended that you contact the Federal Trade Commission in the U.S. (or an equivalent organization in another country), since they can monitor fraud and provide assistance. "Breaches have nothing to do with computers," says Toregas. "They have everything to with your life. They have everything to do with your career, with your credit, with your happiness, with your ability to get on an airplane and not to be arrested for a different identity, and so on."

PART A KEY SKILLS
IDENTIFYING PURPOSE AND TONE

1 Choose the best answer to each question.

1 Which idea best describes the writer's main purpose in writing this article?
  a to warn identity thieves about the possible consequences of their crime
  b to offer information and assistance to victims and potential victims of identity theft
  c to praise effective solutions for identity theft and to criticize ineffective ones

2 What is the main point of paragraph 2?
  a to describe types of online identity theft scams
  b to describe types of help available to victims of a data breach
  c to describe types of services offered by cyber security companies

3 What is the main point of paragraph 3?
  a to explain a service provided for victims by cyber security companies
  b to warn about how a victim's reputation can be harmed
  c to identify ways victims can protect themselves from identity theft

4 Why does the author include a quotation from the expert in the last paragraph?
  a It humanizes a problem that seems to be mostly a technology problem.
  b It reminds readers that identity theft can also affect air travel.
  c It shows how personal happiness is connected to a person's credit and career.

5 What is the overall tone of the article?
  a humorous but serious
  b informative and instructive
  c academic and scholarly

PART B ADDITIONAL SKILLS

2 Complete the sentences.

1 The definition of *data breach* in paragraph 1 is ...
  a a lack of accurate information.
  b the illegal accessing of information.
  c the correction of a mistake.

2 *Surveillance* in paragraph 2 refers to the act of ...
  a punishing someone because they have done something illegal.
  b observing people's behavior because they may be involved in criminal activity.
  c asking people questions to find out the most common opinion about something.

3 *Monitoring* means ...
  a reporting illegal activity to the authorities.
  b making changes to something that is ineffective.
  c watching and checking something carefully over a period of time.

4 If you *clear your name*, you ...
  a avoid identity theft by not using your real name.
  b restore your reputation.
  c hire someone to erase your digital fingerprint.

5 Costis Toregas advises victims of data breaches to ...
  a assume the worst and actively monitor their digital identity.
  b contact the Cyber Security Policy and Research Institute.
  c consult an expert before making changes to their online practices.

Name: _____ Date: _____

PART A KEY VOCABULARY

1 Choose the best word to complete the sentences.

1 The company *regulated / assembled* a strong security team to deal with information breaches.
2 Law enforcement authorities will *violate / prosecute* cybercriminals they catch in court.
3 We will need to *guarantee / eliminate* unnecessary spending this year because of lower profits.
4 It is important for the government to *regulate / guarantee* environmental pollution in our state.
5 Our city's bus service is often *suspended / prosecuted* during snow and ice storms.
6 Although they take many precautions, credit card companies cannot completely *withdraw / guarantee* that their customers' personal information will not be stolen.
7 The administration *violated / eliminated* the constitutional right of its citizens by censoring what was published by journalists.
8 The military plans to *withdraw /suspend* all of its soldiers from the region by the end of the year.

2 Choose the best word to complete the sentences.

1 People who pay their taxes late have to pay a *penalty / humiliation* in addition to the taxes they owe.
2 Reports say that identity theft is on the rise, which is very *malicious /disturbing* news.
3 There is a lot of *validity / barrier* to his ideas on how to stimulate the economy during a depression. We should listen to what he says.
4 When a teacher criticizes a shy student in front of the class, it can cause the student great *humiliation / validity*.
5 Cyberbullies are sometimes difficult to stop because they can remain *anonymous / malicious*.
6 A political conflict between countries can present a *penalty / barrier* to cultural exchange.
7 Emotionally *abusive / anonymous* messages are very harmful for children.
8 My coworker's email to our manager was intentionally *disturbing / malicious*. I think he's trying to get me fired!

PART B LANGUAGE DEVELOPMENT
COLLOCATIONS FOR BEHAVIOR

3 Complete the sentences with the correct form of the expressions in the box.

build a reputation   exhibit good behavior   experience abuse   lose confidence   take responsibility

1 Animals that have _____ will often act aggressively towards people.
2 We usually admire people who _____ for their mistakes and try to make things right.
3 New companies need to _____ for good customer service if they want to succeed.
4 A good teacher knows that students can _____ if exams are unfairly difficult.
5 The best way to teach your children to be polite is to _____ yourself, no matter what the situation.

PROBLEM-SOLUTION COLLOCATIONS

4 Complete the paragraph with the expressions in the box.

becoming an issue   cause problems   confront this challenge   eliminate the risk   poses a threat

Lack of access to fresh water in certain parts of the world is ⁽¹⁾ _____ . For people living in these regions, many of which are in developing countries, this problem ⁽²⁾ _____ to their health and prosperity. When people only have access to low-quality or contaminated water, it can ⁽³⁾ _____ such as disease, poor sanitation, and decreased farming. We must help these communities gain access to clean water in order to stimulate their local economies and ⁽⁴⁾ _____ of ongoing poverty. As we move through the 21st century, it will become increasingly important for us to ⁽⁵⁾ _____ and not leave it for future generations to solve.

Name: _____ Date: _____

PART A GRAMMAR FOR WRITING
IMPERSONAL PASSIVE CONSTRUCTIONS

1 Rewrite the sentences using impersonal passive constructions.

    1 People know that one of the risks of having a credit card is credit card fraud.

    _____

    _____

    2 People understand that identity theft can take many different forms.

    _____

    _____

    3 People say that one should always carefully review credit card statements to check for fraud.

    _____

    _____

    4 People argue that identity theft protection firms can only offer so much protection, and that a risk always remains.

    _____

    _____

    5 People agree that the Federal Trade Commission is a good resource for identity theft victims in the U.S.

    _____

    _____

PASSIVE FOR CONTINUITY

2 Check (✔) the sentences that use the passive form for continuity.

1 Since quality is harder to compare than price, it is not always the first thing thought about when consumers shop.	
2 New food trends are important for restaurants to know about, which is why they are often considered in menu planning.	
3 The thief stole over $10 million worth of artwork before the authorities caught him trying to cross the border into the U.S.	
4 The sun's rays can be harmful to unprotected skin, but people do not always prepare for this when they go to the beach.	
5 Although globalization has improved the lives of people around the world overall, it is regarded by some as a negative influence on society.	

PART B WRITING TASK

> While new technology is often considered positive, it can also introduce problems for its users and society. Describe a type of technology that you think can be problematic, and then explain what you think could be done to improve it.

3 Write a problem-solution essay. Describe the problem, explain its consequences, and write a thesis in the introductory paragraph. Write at least two body paragraphs with possible solutions. Then write a concluding paragraph that refers back to your main idea, emphasizes the importance of acting against this problem, and leaves your readers with something to think about.

Name: _____   Date: _____

PART A KEY SKILLS
SCANNING TO PREVIEW A TEXT

1 Scan the article and indicate whether it is likely to include the information in the chart below.

information desired	yes	no
1 reviews of Airbnb locations		
2 a listing of available temporary jobs		
3 modern alternatives to office jobs		
4 industries embracing "the gig economy"		
5 advantages and disadvantages of freelance work		
6 the growth of independent contractors in the workforce		
7 the tax consequences of being a freelancer		

2 Read the article and answer the questions that follow.

The Gig Economy

1   Technically, the word *gig* means job, but these days it has a special flavor of its own. As linguist Geoff Nunberg states in a National Public Radio commentary, in the 1950s it referred to "any job you took to keep body and soul together while your real life was elsewhere." In other words, a gig was not necessarily part of a career, nor was it work that defined you. In recent years, however, it has come to mean any kind of temporary job. It makes sense, then, that the word is now part of a new work-related term: *the gig economy*. The U.S. Bureau of Labor Statistics (BLS) defines *gig* in this context as "a single project or task for which a worker is hired, often through a digital marketplace, to work on demand." This might include working on one project at a time until each is finished, writing for publications or websites, or having a catering business that operates only when a job is offered. Common fields that employ freelancers include graphic design, information technology, technical writing, and construction. In the U.S., there has been a noticeable rise in this type of work arrangement over the past decade, with the car-sharing companies Uber and Lyft and the home-sharing company Airbnb as some of the most famous new brands of the gig economy.

2   The benefits of this system make it appealing, particularly to young single people. It enables them to choose their own schedules, to limit their work to interesting projects (as long as they earn enough to pay their bills), and to accumulate experience in different kinds of work. Nowadays we often hear about people working for a period and then traveling for a period, and so on. This kind of lifestyle would be impossible for someone working for a company in a fixed full-time position, which usually includes only two or three weeks' vacation per year. Such permanent employees are otherwise expected to be present to make decisions and fulfill ongoing responsibilities. On the other hand, the drawbacks of freelance work are clear: there is much less security than in traditional careers, and there are generally no traditional employee benefits such as private health insurance plans and paid sick days. Furthermore, freelance

incomes tend to fluctuate, which can be stressful. Unfortunately, many people who would prefer a more traditional working life have been forced to take on a collection of lower-paying part-time jobs out of necessity rather than out of a desire for professional freedom. For them, a series of gigs is a minus instead of a plus.

3   It is difficult for the U.S. government to track the number of freelance workers accurately, or the rate of increase in the gig sector. However, data from the Internal Revenue Service (IRS), the government's tax administration, does offer some clues. Most people operating very small, unincorporated businesses with no employees can be classified as members of the gig economy, and between 2003 and 2013 there was notable growth in such "nonemployer businesses" in all industry sectors. In the category not associated with any one industry, called the "other services" sector, there was an increase of nearly 1 million nonemployer businesses during that same period. As the BLS notes on its website, many of the jobs reflected in this last sector would be considered gig employment, such as repair work and individual babysitting jobs. And with the rapid growth of companies like Uber, Lyft, and Airbnb, it appears this business trend will continue to increase on a large scale as the labor force and economy adjust.

PART B ADDITIONAL SKILLS

3 Choose the best answer to each question.

1 Why might the gig economy appeal more to single people than to married people?
   a Freelance work is better for people who have no dependents and fewer responsibilities.
   b Married people don't usually like to travel, and freelance work is best for those who like to travel.
   c Single people can meet other single people more easily doing freelance work.
2 Why might it be stressful to have a fluctuating income?
   a Not ever being able to predict your income could cause worry about savings and bills.
   b Not having the same boss or co-workers all the time could make a worker feel stressed.
   c It could be stressful if some projects pay better but are less interesting than others.
3 Why does the data from the IRS offer clues rather than clear facts about the gig economy?
   a We can only infer that the increases cited are related to gig work.
   b The reading suggests that much of this data is hidden from the IRS.
   c The gig economy is a mysterious topic which has more clues than facts.
4 What increased by about 1 million workers between 2003 and 2013 in the U.S.?
   a nonemployer businesses
   b other services
   c all of the above
5 How would you characterize the overall point of view of this article?
   a It celebrates the gig economy as a necessary and beneficial trend.
   b It is skeptical of the gig economy as a new system.
   c It is a balanced view of the gig economy trend.

Name: _____   Date: _____

PART A KEY VOCABULARY

1 Complete the sentences with the correct form of the words in the box.

> aspiring   component   fluctuate   follow suit
> outweigh   pioneer   retention   transition

1 Certain medications can cause water _____ , which means too much water is kept in your body.
2 Last year, the price of oil _____ greatly, but this year it has become more stable.
3 Bates College made standardized test scores optional for applicants in 1984, and soon other schools _____ and implemented the same policy.
4 The Young People's Writing Workshop offered during the summer is a great opportunity for any _____ authors to gain experience and work with established writers.
5 After six months, we realized that the costs of running the mobile business _____ the profits, so we shut it down.
6 Alexander Fleming was a medical _____ who discovered the use of penicillin to fight bacterial infections.
7 Physical fitness consists of three _____ : strength, endurance, and flexibility.
8 The _____ from being in high school to being in college is huge: there are so many new challenges and experiences to be faced in higher education.

2 Complete the sentences with the correct form of the words in the box.

> accumulate   attainable   break even   incentive
> ongoing   proposition   revenue   shrewdly

1 The government uses the _____ from taxes to pay for the maintenance of roads, bridges, and tunnels.
2 After a difficult start to the semester, I've improved my grades, and I think that a final grade of B in this course is _____ .
3 We had hoped to make a small profit in the first year of our startup, but we only managed to _____ .
4 She invested _____ in alternative energy companies when everyone else was still putting their money into traditional oil businesses, so now she has earned a great deal of money.
5 Because of the _____ conflict in that part of the world, tourism has decreased enormously during the past decade.
6 I started collecting stamps when I was ten years old, and since then I have _____ over 5,000 stamps.
7 Her father said he would buy her a car if her grades improved, which gave her a powerful _____ to study more.
8 We are still considering the _____ from a competitor to purchase our company for $500,000.

PART B LANGUAGE DEVELOPMENT
EXPRESSING CONTRAST

3 Complete the sentences with the contrast signals in the box.

despite   in fact   instead   on the other hand   unlike

1 Although they are similar in appearance, crows like to be around humans, _____ ravens, which prefer the wilderness.

2 _____ their name, Arabic numerals did not originate from the Arabian Peninsula. They were invented in India.

3 It is not true that all mobile businesses earn small profits. _____ , some are very profitable.

4 Studying abroad is a wonderful life experience. _____ , it can also cause homesickness.

5 The flights to Australia were much more expensive than we expected. _____ , we planned a trip to Canada.

BUSINESS AND MARKETING VOCABULARY

4 Complete the paragraph with the correct form of the phrases in the box.

break even   brick-and-mortar generate revenue   start-up costs   turn a profit

If you are thinking about starting a mobile business, there are several steps to follow. First, think of goods or services traditionally sold at a (1)_____ business, like food or haircuts, but which could also be provided from a vehicle.
You will also need to save or borrow enough money in the beginning to cover your (2)_____ . Then, once your business is up and running, work hard and maintain realistic expectations. For example, don't expect to (3)_____ right away; most companies lose money or are lucky to (4)_____ their first year of business. You should be happy if you are able to (5)_____ enough _____ to pay your gas, electricity, and supply costs. Then, as your reputation and customer base grow, you will start to make money in your second year.

Name: _____   Date: _____

PART A GRAMMAR FOR WRITING
REDUCTION OF SUBORDINATE CLAUSES

1   Reduce the first clause to a participial phrase and make any other changes necessary to preserve the original meaning.

   1   While we were planning our new business, we discovered that we were eligible for a special government loan.
   _____
   _____

   2   Because she was trained by an excellent coach, Maria won the race easily.
   _____
   _____

   3   Before he realized that the bus had already left, Tran had run to the station.
   _____
   _____

   4   Since she had been taught Russian by her parents at an early age, Anya was able to communicate with the visitors.
   _____
   _____

   5   I was tired from the long walk, so I decided to take a nap before dinner.
   _____
   _____

PART B WRITING TASK

   Compare and contrast two similar businesses in your community.

2   Write a comparison and contrast report about the two businesses you choose. Think about the products or services they offer, their target market and customers, their staff size, their overhead costs, etc. Use the most appropriate organizational pattern, block or point-by-point, for your report.

Name: _____   Date: _____

Read the article. Then answer the questions that follow.

Brian Wilson: A Beach Boy's Struggles

1   Brian Wilson was born in Los Angeles, California, in 1942. His childhood was difficult, marked by emotional and physical abuse from his father, Murry, but the Wilsons were a musical family, and Brian showed talent even as a boy. As kids, Brian and his brothers Dennis and Carl would sing together and practice vocal harmonies. They used music to escape their painful home life. Soon the brothers, along with their cousin Mike Love, were performing rock and roll music in public. In the early 1960s, they were joined by their high school friend Al Jardine and began calling themselves The Beach Boys. They recorded a single called "Surfin'," which became a radio hit in 1961.

2   With Brian Wilson as their main songwriter and vocal arranger, The Beach Boys recorded many records and appeared in concerts, in movies, and on television during the mid-1960s. They became one of the most successful rock groups of their generation. Wherever you went in the U.S. during the mid-1960s, you were sure to hear The Beach Boys' music on the radio – songs like "Surfin' U.SA.," "California Girls," and "I Get Around." Brian married his girlfriend Marilyn in 1964, and they had two daughters. In 1966 Brian and The Beach Boys created a more sophisticated musical sound with their album *Pet Sounds*. This album is ranked by many music critics among the greatest rock music records ever recorded, and many writers labeled him a genius. Unfortunately, around this time, Brian starting experiment with hallucinogenic drugs, to which he would eventually become addicted.

3   After the release of *Pet Sounds*, Brian began work on another project that he hoped would be an even bigger success. Eventually titled *SMiLE*, he described this album as a "teenage symphony to God." During this time, however, his mental health started to deteriorate. This problem was likely worsened by his drug abuse. Brian was eventually diagnosed with schizophrenia, a very serious mental illness. During this period, he suffered numerous nervous breakdowns, refused to leave his house, and told people he could hear voices in his head. He finished the *SMiLE* album, but both his band and his record company rejected it because they thought it was too strange sounding to release.

4   In the 1980s, Wilson began seeing psychologists and working hard to improve his mental health. He stopped using illegal drugs, tried different therapies, and slowly began to improve. By the mid-1990s he had returned to releasing albums and performing live music regularly. In 2004, *SMiLE* was finally released. In 2012, Brian toured the world with The Beach Boys to celebrate their 50th anniversary as a band. In 2015, he became the subject of a biographical film titled *Love & Mercy*.

5   What had triggered Brian's mental illness? He contends it was probably a combination of genetic factors, the abuse that he suffered as a child, and his drug abuse. Today, although he continues to live with mental illness, he is able to have a productive and busy life. He has said, "I think in terms of emotions. And feelings. So sometimes what I say may not always be clear. But creatively, there's a lot to be said for that way of thinking."

PART A GENERAL SKILLS

1 Choose the best answer to each question.

1 Why do you think the group called themselves The Beach Boys?
    a because they met at the beach
    b because California is famous for its beach culture
    c because they wanted to escape from their home life

2 What does the adjective *sophisticated* mean in paragraph 2?
    a easy to sing
    b difficult to understand
    c complex and detailed

3 What does the verb *deteriorate* mean in paragraph 3?
    a to worsen
    b to become stable
    c to improve

4 Which factor is cited as contributing to Brian Wilson's mental illness?
    a drug abuse
    b stress
    c a bad marriage
    d musical disagreements with his band

5 How would you characterize the final paragraph of the article?
    a giving a warning
    b expressing optimism
    c making a prediction

PART B KEY SKILLS
USING GRAPHIC ORGANIZERS TO TAKE NOTES

2 Complete the notes with details from the article.

Brian Wilson's successes	Brian Wilson's struggles
– (1) 1st hit song:	– (8) father:
– (2) mid–1960s:	– (9) addiction:
– (3) Pet Sounds:	– (10) mental illness:
– (4) family:	– (11) SMiLE:
– (5) 1990s:	
– (6) 2004:	
– (7) 2012:	

INTERPRETING QUOTES

3 Read the quotations and choose the better interpretation.

1 "I think in terms of emotions. And feelings. So sometimes what I say may not always be clear. But creatively, there's a lot to be said for that way of thinking." – *Brian Wilson*
   a We don't always have to understand great art in order to have an emotional response to it.
   b Some artists concentrate on emotions and feelings in their art, while others do not.

2 "Bad times make good art." – *anonymous*
   a When life is difficult, it can stimulate creative people to respond with especially interesting art.
   b When life is difficult, it can help us to see beautiful art and feel better.

3 "Although the world is full of suffering, it is also full of the overcoming of it." – *Helen Keller*
   a When bad things in the world upset you, you can choose to focus on the good things happening as well, such as the arts or advances in medicine.
   b Suffering in this world can take many forms, such as physical pain, emotional pain, and poverty, but if you are patient, all suffering will end.

4 "Be the change you want to see in the world." – *Mahatma Gandhi*
   a The world has always changed and will continue to do so, no matter what we do.
   b It is best to try and improve what you feel needs to change yourself.

5 "The goal of life is living in agreement with nature." – *Zeno, ancient Greek philosopher*
   a In everything we do we must maintain respect for the earth.
   b Humans are responsible for environmental problems like climate change and pollution.

Name: _____   Date: _____

PART A KEY VOCABULARY

1   Complete the sentences with the correct form of the words in the box.

innovative   intriguing   norm   reject   resourceful   seek   skeptical   stimulation

1   That artist makes _____ use of materials not traditionally associated with art.
2   After so much mental and physical _____ at the amusement park, the children could hardly stay awake for dinner.
3   In Japan, bowing and presenting business cards to one another is the _____ .
4   Although the musician initially _____ the doctor's diagnosis of depression, his family convinced him that he had a problem and needed treatment.
5   The plot of the new movie sounds unusual and _____ . I can't wait to see it this weekend.
6   When you have very little money, you have to be _____ and figure out how to make things last.
7   If you notice unusual discoloring or growths on your skin, you should _____ treatment as soon as possible.
8   Although I was _____ at first about her qualifications for the job, she quickly established herself as the most important member of our team.

2   Complete the sentences with the correct form of the words in the box.

breakthrough   confirm   label   notion procrastinator   pursue   suppress   trigger

1   The scientist's discovery proved to be an important medical _____ that led to a new cancer treatment and saved many lives.
2   Sadly, in the past, autistic children were often _____ as untreatable and were locked away in mental hospitals.
3   We called the hotel to _____ our reservation for next week.
4   The significant reduction of state health funding to medical clinics _____ the worst outbreak of flu in the state's history.
5   Parents should encourage creativity in their children and never _____ it, since it is an important part of intellectual growth.
6   Jim should be finishing his assignment tonight, but he's such a _____ that he will probably go out with his friends instead.
7   Some people think that having a woman change her last name when she gets married is an old-fashioned _____ .
8   My sister plans to _____ a career as an attorney, so she is applying to law school.

PART B LANGUAGE DEVELOPMENT
EXPERIMENTAL SCIENCE TERMINOLOGY

3 Complete the paragraph with the correct form of the words and phrases in the box.

conduct a study   contend   establish a causal link   implication   research subject

It has long been a common practice to use animals such as mice as (1)_____ in order to test the effects of new foods and medicines before administering anything to humans. For example, several decades ago, food scientists (2)_____ on the effects of eating an artificial sweetener called cyclamate. They wanted to see if they could (3)_____ between cyclamate and cancer. In other words, they suspected that eating cyclamate might lead to cancer. In fact, they found that large amounts of cyclamate did cause cancer in the mice. In their report, the scientists (4)_____ that their results had serious (5)_____ for the health of humans as well.

UNIT 5 WRITING QUIZ

Name: _____   Date: _____

PART A GRAMMAR FOR WRITING
COMPLEX NOUN PHRASES WITH *WHAT*

1   Rewrite the sentences so that they contain a complex noun phrase with *what*. Make sure to use the correct form of the verb after *what*.

1   The things that are considered to comprise creativity can differ from person to person.

_____

_____

2   People often do not realize that mental illness can be treated with effective medication.

_____

_____

3   The aspect of this museum that I like most is the wonderful collection of 20th-century art.

_____

_____

4   The thing that we need to realize is that it can be tough to make a living as an artist.

_____

_____

5   One of the reasons many people like Vincent Van Gogh's paintings is the way that he used color.

_____

_____

PART B WRITING TASK

Is photography art? Find several sources for both sides of the argument.

2   Write an explanatory synthesis essay in which you present the main arguments on both sides of the prompt. Be sure to cite your sources and quotations properly.

Name: _____   Date: _____

PART A KEY SKILLS
INTERPRETING GRAPHICAL INFORMATION

1 You are going to read an essay about internships. Look at the graph. Answer the questions based on the information in the graph.

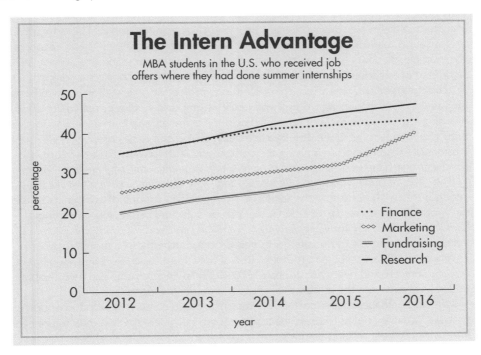

1 Which sector experienced the greatest increase in full-time job offers for interns between 2012 and 2016? _____

2 What year did all four sectors record the highest percentage of full-time job offers for interns? _____

3 Interns hired for which sector received the highest percentage of job offers? _____

4 What happened to job offers for marketing interns between 2015 and 2016?

_____

5 What is true about the percentage of job offers to former interns in the finance and research sectors from 2012–2013? _____

6 What general trend is shown by the graph? _____

_____

2 Read the essay. Then answer the questions that follow.

The Value of Unpaid Internships

1   College students looking to the future and thinking about their careers often consider the practical aspects of a job like salary, benefits, and opportunities for promotion. But for those who are in the process of getting their degrees, finding work in a competitive chosen field upon graduation can be difficult. One way to gain an advantage prior to finishing their studies is for students to consider using their breaks – winter, spring, and summer vacations or gap years – for internships, even if they are unpaid. Although the idea of working for free might not appeal, the benefits of these internships are clear. They provide students with work experience that would be hard to find otherwise, they help students become accustomed to the working world, and they give invaluable networking opportunities.

2   The fact is that for many careers, there is no substitute for real-world work experience. For example, students who plan to work in business, finance, or marketing cannot get the same kind of experience in a classroom that they can get by working for a company. Having actual responsibilities that affect the success of a project or organization is much better preparation for the working world than merely writing case studies or reading textbooks. This alone justifies the value of an unpaid position. After all, an intern generally does not bring experience to his or her role in a company. So, in reality, the company is giving the intern more than the intern is giving the company, at least initially. The interns, on the other hand, get first-hand knowledge and experience in a specific company and role for free.

3   The value of unpaid internships goes beyond work experience in one firm. More generally, many students find the transition from the daily routine of college life to the daily routine of a career to be a shock that can be softened by previous internships. Dressing appropriately for work, arriving to work on time, and following the pattern of a daily job are difficult to prepare for in a classroom. Furthermore, a professional work environment requires a person to follow instructions from supervisors and learn how to communicate and negotiate duties with coworkers. An internship can help people understand and learn these "soft skills" before entering the workplace.

4   Last, and perhaps most importantly, internships provide students with the opportunity to make valuable contacts – business associates who can help them in their future careers. Interns who work hard and demonstrate potential and ability in their chosen field will find colleagues who are willing to advocate for them and provide recommendations, perhaps even hire them after graduation. While recommendations from professors are helpful, from a future employer's perspective, there is no substitute for professional recommendations and connections.

5   The idea of working for free during vacations may be distasteful, but once the benefits are taken into account, the value is clear. While a good education is obviously important, it is not sufficient to prepare students for the competitive working world. An internship can help address that knowledge gap and build students' expertise before they start their careers. Excelling at an internship should be like getting good grades in school – something every student should strive for and take seriously.

PART B ADDITIONAL SKILLS

3 Choose the best answer to each question.

1 What does the essay suggest about unpaid internships?
   a All students understand why it is a valuable experience.
   b Some students may not see the value and dislike working for free.
   c Most students do unpaid internships during their summer break.

2 What is true about the essay?
   a The author admits that unpaid internships may seem unfair on the surface.
   b The author focuses on the benefits and future advantages of unpaid internships.
   c The author prefers unpaid internships to paid internships.

3 What is the meaning of *networking* in paragraph 1?
   a a computer system that connects people in the same office
   b an exchange of ideas
   c building a set of personal connections

4 What is the focus of paragraph 4?
   a the relationship between interns and coworkers
   b the relationship between teachers and students
   c the relationship between managers and employees

5 How would you characterize the style of this essay?
   a an argumentative essay with a point of view
   b an objective description of a phenomenon
   c an explanatory synthesis of various sources

UNIT 6 LANGUAGE QUIZ

Name: _____   Date: _____

PART A KEY VOCABULARY

1 Complete the sentences with the correct form of the words in the box.

alternative   ambiguity   boast   dispute
persistent   potential   qualified   survey

1 My brother still _____ that he was the best basketball player in his high school, but I think his best friend was better.
2 We had planned to have a picnic in the park, but because it was raining we had to make a(n) _____ plan.
3 After three weeks I finally went to the doctor for some medicine to cure this _____ cough.
4 Jana was much more _____ than the other applicants, which is why she got the job.
5 The information in the graph is based on an online _____ of more than 10,000 social media users.
6 I had to ask Anita to clarify her plan because of the _____ of some of the details.
7 The company charged in the lawsuit is not _____ that they did something wrong, but they are questioning the actual damage that resulted from their actions.
8 We are hopeful about our financial future because the new governor's policies have the _____ to improve the state's tax system.

2 Complete the sentences with the correct form of the words in the box.

assertive   chronic   diminish   expertise
extend   founder   illustration   prospective

1 Some illnesses, such as diabetes, are _____ , and require patients to manage them their entire life.
2 Jim has a lot of _____ in website design, which is why he was chosen to lead the Media department.
3 His _____ personality enabled him to convince others and make the necessary changes.
4 The problems we have been having with our delivery service are a(n) _____ of why we need to improve our customer service.
5 The recent rainfall does not _____ the fact that the region is still in the middle of a severe drought.
6 The bank agreed to _____ the deadline for my loan by six months.
7 Elon Musk is the _____ and driving force behind a number of companies, including SpaceX, Tesla Inc., and SolarCity.
8 In addition to the job interview, all _____ applicants will have to undergo a day of psychological and mathematical testing.

          Prism 4 Reading and Writing © Cambridge University Press 2017 **Photocopiable**

PART B LANGUAGE DEVELOPMENT
COMPLEX NOUN PHRASES

3 Choose a word or phrase from each box to complete the sentences.

job   information   training
work-life   household

balance   income   market
program   technology

1 My degree in computer science helped me find a position in the bank's
   _____ department after graduation.
2 The vocational school has an excellent _____ at a local hospital for
   people studying to be nurses.
3 According to a government website, the country's median _____
   was $51,939 in 2014.
4 My new job provides a better _____ than the last one, because now
   I can be home for dinner with my family every night.
5 The global recession and the weak _____ in 2008 made it difficult for
   many college students to find work after graduating.

Name: _____   Date: _____

PART A GRAMMAR FOR WRITING
ACTIVE VS. PASSIVE VOICE TO DISCUSS FIGURES

1   Complete the sentences with the correct form of the verbs in parentheses.

  1   The results of the survey _____ (show) in Figure 3.
  2   This data clearly _____ (support) the notion that unemployment is down from last year.
  3   The decrease in overall wages _____ (demonstrate) by the blue line in the chart.
  4   The graph below _____ (indicate) that most Americans receive health insurance from their employers.
  5   As the information in Figure 1 _____ (suggest), median salaries are expected to increase gradually in the next five years.

PART B WRITING TASK

> Is it better to be self-employed (a freelancer) or to work full-time for a company?

2   Write an argumentative essay that answers the question in the writing prompt. Include a clear thesis statement that expresses your opinion. Provide specific details and examples to support your view. If possible, find and use information from a graph or other figure to support at least one of your points.

Name: _____ Date: _____

Read the article. The answer the questions that follow.

The Zika Virus

1   *Zika* is a virus that has been in the news of late. The peak spread of a recent Zika outbreak occurred between 2014 and 2016. People are infected with Zika by means of infected mosquitoes. The mosquitoes responsible for transmitting the virus were found throughout the Americas as far north as Florida and Texas in the United States. In fact, the *Aedes aegypti* type of mosquito was reported to be in every country in North, Central, and South America except for Canada and Chile. While Zika can also be contracted through sexual contact with an infected person, the best way to protect against getting the virus is to avoid mosquito bites. Some ways to counter mosquito bites include using insect repellant on exposed skin, wearing long-sleeved shirts and long pants, staying indoors or inside screened areas, and removing standing water around the home, conditions where mosquitoes are known to breed.

2   Perhaps the most troubling result of the Zika virus is that infected pregnant women can give birth to babies with birth defects. One defect in particular, called *microcephaly*, causes babies to be born with underdeveloped brains and undersized heads. Brazil was among the countries hit particularly hard with this phenomenon. Other birth defects that have been observed are developmental delays and different forms of paralysis. In the worst cases, some infants have even died from Zika.

3   For this reason, the U.S. Centers for Disease Control and Prevention (the CDC) issued guidelines in 2016 for potential prospective parents to follow. According to these guidelines, women diagnosed with the Zika virus or showing symptoms such as rash, fever, and joint pain, should delay trying to get pregnant for at least eight weeks. Women who have visited a Zika-infected area but who do not exhibit symptoms of the Zika virus should also wait at least eight weeks before trying to get pregnant. For men, the CDC recommends waiting at least six months after their symptoms first appear before trying to get their partner pregnant. This is because the virus can survive in men's bodies longer than in women's bodies. The CDC further urges those who have been exposed to the virus to use protection during sexual activity.

4   Fortunately, there is evidence that instances of Zika virus are diminishing. Nevertheless, the CDC recommends that people traveling to infected areas be very careful and follow the guidelines presented here. It may not be possible to eradicate the Zika virus completely, but its spread can be controlled to varying degrees.

PART A KEY SKILLS
RECOGNIZING DISCOURSE ORGANIZATION

1 Choose the best answer for each question.

1 What discourse organization does the author use in paragraph 1?
   a She identifies a problem and lists some solutions.
   b She gives an opinion and provides evidence for that opinion.
   c She presents a counterargument to an opposing argument.

2 What purpose does the phrase "in fact" serve in paragraph 1?
   a It contradicts the statement that comes before it.
   b It makes the following statement seem more scientific.
   c It adds more specific information to the previous statement.

3 What reason does the writer refer to in the first sentence of paragraph 3?
   a the danger of travelling to Brazil
   b the danger of giving birth to a baby with defects
   c the danger of getting pregnant when infected with Zika

4 What comparison is made in paragraph 3?
   a the length of time women who show symptoms and women who visit infected areas should wait to get pregnant
   b the length of time Zika can survive in men and women
   c the effectiveness of the 2016 CDC guidelines and previously published guidelines

5 Why does the author use the word "nevertheless" in paragraph 4?
   a to emphasize that the dangers of Zika virus are decreasing
   b to emphasize that the dangers of Zika still exist
   c to contradict the idea that the spread of Zika is declining

PART B ADDITIONAL SKILLS

2 Read the statements. Write T (true), F (false), or DNS (does not say). Correct the false statements.

_____ 1 Zika virus has not been found in Canada.
_____

_____ 2 People can contract Zika virus from mosquitoes and also from other people.
_____

_____ 3 The Zika virus will likely spread to Europe in the near future.
_____

_____ 4 Microcephaly has only been found in babies in Brazil.
_____

_____ 5 The CDC publishes guidelines for protection against all outbreaks of diseases in the Americas.
_____

_____ 6 The Zika virus affects more women than men.
_____

_____ 7 Zika is expected to disappear soon.
_____

Prism 4 Reading and Writing © Cambridge University Press 2017 **Photocopiable**

UNIT 7 LANGUAGE QUIZ

Name: _____   Date: _____

PART A KEY VOCABULARY

1 Complete the sentences with the correct form of the words in the box.

> bounce back   cycle   eradicate   grim
> mild   proximity   surge   transmission

1 The _____ of the seasons is always the same: winter, spring, summer, and autumn.
2 Small pox is the only infectious disease affecting humans that has officially been _____ , with the last known case having been identified in 1977.
3 After several months of bad health, my grandmother has _____ and returned to her usual activities.
4 Unfortunately, babies born with microcephaly face _____ futures; they usually experience serious health problems for the rest of their lives.
5 This town is a popular place for families to live because of its _____ to a major city.
6 Although she had a cold, it was fairly _____ , so she was able to keep working.
7 There has been a _____ in hate crimes since the election, which is causing concern for the police and citizens alike.
8 The _____ of certain viruses, such as Zika, is by insect bites.

2 Complete the sentences with the correct form of the words in the box.

> confine   counter   detection   domesticated
> facilitate   revolutionize   therapeutic   thrive

1 After he was criticized for his inhumane policies, the politician _____ with unfounded accusations of bias in the media.
2 Even if it is possible for them to be _____ , wild animals should not be kept as pets.
3 Pregnant women are sometimes _____ to their beds by their doctors until time for the baby to arrive.
4 Some psychiatrists think that this drug has _____ value for the mentally ill, while others feel that more testing is needed before prescribing it to their patients.
5 The discovery of penicillin by Alexander Fleming in 1928 _____ the treatment of bacterial infections, changing the world of medicine completely.
6 The early _____ of certain cancers can dramatically improve a patient's chances of overcoming the disease.
7 The new law will _____ the ability of health officials to help low-income families by making it easier to sign them up for health insurance and preventive care.
8 Studies have shown that most students _____ in a classroom where they are encouraged to be creative and to express and test their ideas.

PART B LANGUAGE DEVELOPMENT
VERBS AND VERB PHRASES FOR CAUSATION

3 Choose the correct answers to complete the sentences.

1 The health of the mother can *affect / encourage* the health of her baby.
2 The government needs to *impact / promote* healthy lifestyles so that public health costs are kept low.
3 Public anger over the president's attempts to intimidate the press *enabled / triggered* huge protests across the country.
4 A healthy diet *drives / is a factor in* the length of a person's life.
5 The manager of our department *permits / has an effect on* us to leave work early on Fridays.

WORD FAMILIES

4 Complete the sentences with the correct form of the words in parentheses.

1 Catching and treating the virus as early as possible is the best way to _____ an outbreak. (preventive)
2 The _____ of bird flu from chickens to humans is quite rare. (transmit)
3 After tearing his Achilles tendon, the athlete needed months of physical _____ before he could start training again. (therapeutic)
4 It is important to clean and treat serious wounds with antibiotics so that they do not become _____ . (infection)
5 There is a stereotype that older people are more _____ to change than younger people. (resist)

Name: _____   Date: _____

PART A GRAMMAR IN WRITING
CAUSE AND EFFECT: LOGICAL CONNECTORS

1 Complete the sentences with the correct form of the words or phrases in the box.

> as a consequence   because   due to   result in   so that

1 A poor diet often _____ health problems.
2 _____ it is dangerous to take too much medication, patients must always follow the directions carefully.
3 Many medical health professionals worked to eradicate smallpox. _____ , it is no longer a health threat.
4 After his operation, my father started exercising every day _____ he would be in better physical condition.
5 Some people who need medical attention cannot get it _____ the fact that they have no health insurance.

PART B WRITING TASK

> How do lifestyle choices affect long-term health?

2 Write an essay that explains the causes and potential effects of a lifestyle choice on a person's health. Choose a lifestyle choice that is generally thought to be negative (smoking, poor diet, lack of exercise, etc). Provide recommendations for changes a person could make that would lead to better health.

Name: _____ Date: _____

Read the article. Then answer the questions that follow.

Freelancing

1   The **etymology** of the term "freelance" is the combination of two words: "free," meaning independent, and "lance," referring to a weapon. The original freelancer was a soldier who was available for hire by whichever person or nation was willing to pay him the most. In modern times, the term has evolved to mean a self-employed person who works for various companies on a short-term or project-by-project basis. Freelancers are writers, project managers, corporate consultants, or even doctors and nurses. Though typically only an option for highly experienced workers in the past, these days freelancing has become a popular option for people just entering the job market. Even so, it is important to examine the pros and cons of freelancing carefully before choosing this option.

2   The benefits of freelance work are many: choosing when and where you want to work, declining jobs or projects that don't appeal to you, having the opportunity to collaborate with many different workers, supervisors, and organizations, and perhaps being able to apply your skills in different industries and areas of the world. Freelancers can usually choose the work schedule that best suits them. After all, some people work best in the morning; others work best at night. Household chores, lunch dates, and doctors' appointments can be scheduled for **whenever it suits them**. Freelancers often have less or no commuting needs, and, depending on the task, they might not even have to be at home to do their work. Coffee shops are often dotted with freelancers on laptops. And if a freelancer is offered work that is not appealing, they can turn it down – if doing so is an affordable option, that is. Probably the most popular benefit of freelancing, though, is variety. Freelancers often get to collaborate with more people and with more different types of companies than someone working with the same people at the same location every day. This can make the **daily grind** of work life more interesting and help people expand their professional network.

3   There are, of course, disadvantages to being a freelancer as well. Freelancers have no predictable salary to rely on. Plus, there are usually administrative tasks unrelated to their main occupation that must be done, tasks that might be done for them if they were working full time for a company. Such tasks could include billing and paying invoices, photocopying, and handling paperwork, which, particularly for **creative types** like graphic designers, might be stressful and frustrating. In addition, freelancers are always looking for their next job, and also thinking about how much they are earning from their current work. Is it enough, or should they take on more in order to pay the bills? Finally, being a freelancer is a huge responsibility. Instead of having the support of a boss, they are the boss. The praise and credit for the work is all theirs, but so too is all the blame or criticism. **The buck stops with them**. This degree of individual responsibility can feel like isolation for some people.

4   In short, working as a freelancer can be a wonderful, satisfying career choice, but it is not the right choice for everyone. Understanding the pros and cons is important for anyone who is considering becoming a freelancer, either as a first career move or by making the move from a full- or part-time position to becoming their own boss.

PART A KEY SKILLS
USING CONTEXT CLUES

1 Find the words in bold in the article. Then use context clues to answer the questions.

  1 What is the **etymology** of a word?
    a its origin and history
    b its pronunciation and spelling
    c its modern definition

  2 How can the expression **whenever it suits them** best be paraphrased?
    a anytime you feel something is appropriate, based on what is customary
    b anytime you are forced to do something, based on your responsibilities
    c anytime you feel like doing something, based on what seems right to you

  3 What is the meaning of the **daily grind**?
    a lunch break
    b routine
    c excitement

  4 What are **creative types** in this context?
    a artistic people
    b freelancers
    c administrative assistants

  5 What is the best way to interpret the idiom **the buck stops with them**?
    a They are the boss, and the boss makes all of the final decisions.
    b Their clients, not the freelancers, have the final decision-making responsibility.
    c They should only accept U.S. dollars as payment for services.

PART B ADDITIONAL SKILLS

2 Answer the questions.

  1 What are two examples of freelancers mentioned in the article?

    _____

  2 What are two benefits of freelance work?

    _____

  3 What are two drawbacks of freelance work?

    _____

  4 Who is probably the intended audience for this article?

    _____

  5 What is the main point of the article?

    _____

Name: _____ Date: _____

PART A KEY VOCABULARY

1 Complete the sentences with the correct form of the words in the box.

> accomplish   apparently   coordinate   decline
> detract from   distraction   gesture   underlie

1 The most important thing he _____ as CEO was to turn the company around so that it consistently made a profit after years of losing money.
2 The hope is that this birthday party will be a nice _____ from all the stress we've been under lately.
3 I thought that she was a freelancer, but _____ she works here full time because I see her in the office every day.
4 The fact that he wears glasses does not _____ his handsomeness. In fact, it makes him better looking.
5 As a _____ of respect, I let the boss choose which chair to sit in before I sat down.
6 The country's economic problems _____ all of the other challenges facing us right now.
7 The sales department needs to _____ with the marketing department so that the schedule for the project can be planned out for the next three years.
8 Unfortunately, my grandfather's health has _____ , and he is back in the hospital.

2 Complete the sentences with the correct form of the words in the box.

> consistent   differentiate   display   enhance
> exclusively   fundamental   isolate   phenomenon

1 People with the flu _____ certain symptoms, like headaches, congestion, and tiredness.
2 The format of the document has to be _____ with the format of the other documents in the series.
3 That annoying sound seems to be coming from everywhere! Can you please _____ the source and make it stop?
4 Adding a little bit of salt to sweet things will _____ the flavor.
5 Jennifer's twin decided to get a haircut in order to _____ her appearance from her sister's.
6 Using social media to find a date is a modern _____ that my grandparents do not understand.
7 This MBA program is _____ for people who want to focus on finance. It is not for those interested in general business.
8 Understanding how cells work is a _____ concept of biology.

PART B LANGUAGE DEVELOPMENT
HEDGING

3 Rewrite the italicized sections of the student's paragraph so that they are hedged statements.

Here are a few observations about Italy, based on the month I spent in Venice. First, [1] *everyone thinks* that Italy is a wonderful place to visit or live. Its scenery, history, architecture, and food are [2] *loved by everyone*. [3] *Italians eat* a lot of cheese, meat, and pasta. If you decide to travel there, [4] *you will definitely love it*. Finally, unlike other parts of the world, [5] *Italy is a rich country*.

1 _____

2 _____

3 _____

4 _____

5 _____

UNIT 8 WRITING QUIZ

Name: _____ Date: _____

PART A GRAMMAR FOR WRITING
ACKNOWLEDGMENT AND CONCESSION

1 Read each statement and underline the language of acknowledgment or concession. Then use logical connectors to write a counterargument.

  1 Many people think that the legal drinking age in the U.S. should be lowered to 18, when people are allowed to vote and serve in the military.

  _____
  _____

  2 Testing of medication on animals may provide important health information.

  _____
  _____

  3 It is true that the government takes a lot of tax money out of its citizens' paychecks.

  _____
  _____

  4 Some children may be motivated to get better grades if their parents give them money as a reward.

  _____
  _____

  5 There is no doubt that some students feel homesick when they study abroad.

  _____
  _____

PART B WRITING TASK

> Do you agree or disagree with the following statement? "Collaboration with other people always results in the greatest possible success in any project." Use reasons and examples to support your answer.

2 Write an argumentative essay. Include at least one counterargument to your position and explain why it is not true or not accurate.

Prism 4 Reading and Writing © Cambridge University Press 2017 **Photocopiable**

UNIT QUIZZES ANSWER KEY

UNIT 1 READING QUIZ
PART A KEY SKILLS

1 1 a 2 c 3 a

2 1 a 2 c 3 b

3 1 b, c 2 a, b, c 3 b, c, f 4 b

PART B ADDITIONAL SKILLS

3 1 c 2 b 3 a 4 b 5 c

UNIT 1 LANGUAGE QUIZ
PART A KEY VOCABULARY

1 1 practice 2 prompted 3 vulnerable
4 deliberate 5 recover 6 emerged
7 memorabilia 8 capacity

2 1 developer 2 vacant 3 deteriorating
4 maintains 5 renovations 6 facilities
7 affordable 8 prosper

PART B LANGUAGE DEVELOPMENT

3 1 at the turn of the century
2 slowly but surely
3 at one time
4 out of date
5 for the time being

4 a well-known b low-income c fast-growing
d up to date e long-term

UNIT 1 WRITING QUIZ
PART A GRAMMAR FOR WRITING

1 1 U 2 R 3 R 4 U 5 R

PART B WRITING TASK

2 *Answers will vary.*

UNIT 2 READING QUIZ
PART A KEY SKILLS

1 1 price 2 product innovation 3 sales goals
4 expensive 5 competition 6 bankruptcy
7 playful image 8 set up 9 use 10 "Think
Different" campaign 11 famous innovative people
12 posters 13 tablets 14 Apple, Inc. 15 most
valuable brand

2 1 a 2 b 3 c 4 a 5 b

PART B ADDITIONAL SKILLS

3 1 a 2 b 3 c 4 a 5 b

UNIT 2 LANGUAGE QUIZ
PART A KEY VOCABULARY

1 1 devoted to 2 subsequent 3 resemble
4 appropriate 5 opposition to 6 resist
7 contemporary 8 criteria

2 1 retained 2 associate 3 evolved 4 donations
5 human rights 6 modify 7 appeal to 8 opt for

PART B LANGUAGE DEVELOPMENT

3 1 outrage 2 trouble 3 awe 4 suspicion
5 emotions

4 *Answers will vary. Possible answers:*
1 If marketers target their ads for older generations,
the children and grandchildren of those people are
not unlikely to be impressed.
2 Simply updating a logo or slogan is not sufficient
for a company to rebrand itself in the eyes
of consumers.
3 Providing free samples on campuses is an effective
strategy for introducing new personal care products
to college-aged consumers.
4 The purpose of rebranding can vary from company
to company. Some businesses do so to stop
declining sales; others looking to improve existing
sales of an established product.
5 Good logos do not require many different elements
or colors. Some of the best known ones are simple
and monochromatic.

UNIT 2 WRITING QUIZ
PART A GRAMMAR FOR WRITING

1 1 Nike's logo, which is sometimes called the "swoosh,"
is recognized around the world. / Nike's logo, which
is recognized around the world, is sometimes called
the "swoosh."
2 More and more companies are emphasizing
environmental friendliness, which is important to
consumers, in their marketing. / Environmental
friendliness, which is important to consumers, is
being emphasized by companies more and more.
3 Marketing a product, which includes many different
ways to get attention for it, can be quite expensive.

4 Apple, which successfully rebranded itself in the 1990s, is now considered the most valuable company in the world.

5 The target market for PCs, which now includes practically everyone, used to be mostly male customers.

2 1 A slogan, a company's marketing phrase, can be a key part of a successful marketing campaign.

2 Warby Parker, an eyewear retailer, found success by selling inexpensive yet fashionable glasses. / Eyewear retailer Warby Parker found success by selling inexpensive yet fashionable glasses.

3 John Pemberton, an Atlanta pharmacist, developed the original formula for Coca-Cola in the 19th century. / Atlanta pharmacist John Pemberton developed the original formula for Coca-Cola in the 19th century.

4 SoulCycle, a New York-based fitness company, has had great success in marketing exercise as fun and friendship instead of work. / New York-based fitness company SoulCycle has had great success in marketing exercise as fun and friendship instead of work.

5 The Harry Potter books, international bestsellers, were originally marketed to children and young adults only.

PART B WRITING TASK

3 *Answers will vary.*

UNIT 3 READING QUIZ
PART A KEY SKILLS

1 1 b   2 c   3 c   4 a   5 b

PART B ADDITIONAL SKILLS

2 1 b   2 b   3 c   4 b   5 a

UNIT 3 LANGUAGE QUIZ
PART A KEY VOCABULARY

1 1 assembled   2 prosecute   3 eliminate
4 regulate   5 suspended   6 guarantee
7 violated   8 withdraw

2 1 penalty   2 disturbing   3 validity   4 humiliation
5 anonymous   6 barrier   7 abusive   8 malicious

PART B LANGUAGE DEVELOPMENT

3 1 experienced abuse   2 take responsibility
3 build a reputation   4 lose confidence
5 exhibit good behavior

4 1 becoming an issue   2 poses a threat
3 cause problems   4 eliminate the risk
5 confront this challenge

UNIT 3 WRITING QUIZ
PART A GRAMMAR FOR WRITING

1 1 It is known that one of the risks of having a credit card is credit card fraud. / Credit card fraud is known to be one of the risks of having a credit card.

2 It is understood that identity theft can take many different forms. / Identity theft is understood to take many different forms.

3 It is said that one should always carefully review credit card statements to check for fraud. / It is said that credit card statements should always be carefully reviewed to check for fraud.

4 It is argued that identity-theft-protection firms can only offer so much protection, and that a risk always remains.

5 It is agreed that the Federal Trade Commission is a good resource for identity theft victims in the U.S. / The Federal Trade Commission is agreed to be a good resource for identity theft victims in the U.S.

2 1, 2, 5

PART B WRITING TASK

3 *Answers will vary.*

UNIT 4 READING QUIZ
PART A KEY SKILLS

1 1 no   2 no   3 yes   4 yes   5 yes   6 yes   7 no

PART B ADDITIONAL SKILLS

3 1 a   2 a   3 a   4 b   5 c

UNIT 4 LANGUAGE QUIZ
PART A KEY VOCABULARY

1 1 retention   2 fluctuated   3 followed suit
4 aspiring   5 outweighed   6 pioneer
7 components   8 transition

2 1 revenue   2 attainable   3 break even   4 shrewdly
5 ongoing   6 accumulated   7 incentive
8 proposition

PART B LANGUAGE DEVELOPMENT

3 1 unlike   2 Despite   3 In fact
4 On the other hand   5 Instead

4 1 brick-and-mortar   2 start-up costs
3 turn a profit   4 break even   5 generate revenue

UNIT 4 WRITING QUIZ
PART A GRAMMAR FOR WRITING

1 1 While planning our new business, we discovered that we were eligible for a special government loan.
  2 Trained by an excellent coach, Maria won the race easily. / Having been trained by an excellent coach, Maria won the race easily.
  3 Before realizing that the bus had already left, Tran had run to the station.
  4 Taught Russian by her parents at an early age, Anya was able to communicate with the visitors.
  5 Tired from the long walk, I decided to take a nap before dinner.

PART B WRITING TASK

2 *Answers will vary.*

UNIT 5 READING QUIZ
PART A GENERAL SKILLS

1 1 b 2 c 3 a 4 a 5 b

PART B KEY SKILLS

2 1 "Surfin" (1961)
  2 Concerts, movies, TV, radio hits
  3 more sophisticated, critics love it
  4 wife and two daughters
  5 returned to making music
  6 *SMiLE* album released
  7 50th anniversary world tour
  8 father abusive
  9 hallucinogenic drugs
  10 schizophrenia, nervous breakdown
  11 band and label initially rejected; released years later

3 1 a 2 a 3 a 4 b 5 a

UNIT 5 LANGUAGE QUIZ
PART A KEY VOCABULARY

1 1 innovative 2 stimulation 3 norm 4 rejected
  5 intriguing 6 resourceful 7 seek 8 skeptical

2 breakthrough 2 labeled 3 confirm 4 triggered
  5 suppress 6 procrastinator 7 notion 8 pursue

PART B LANGUAGE DEVELOPMENT

3 1 research subjects 2 conducted a study
  3 establish a causal link 4 contend/contended
  5 implications

UNIT 5 WRITING QUIZ
PART A GRAMMAR FOR WRITING

1 1 What is considered to comprise creativity can differ from person to person.
  2 What people often do not realize is that mental illness can be treated with effective medication.
  3 What I like most about this museum is the wonderful collection of 20th-century art.
  4 What we need to realize is that it can be tough to make a living as an artist.
  5 What many people like about Vincent Van Gogh's paintings is the way (that) he used color.

PART B WRITING TASK

2 *Answers will vary.*

UNIT 6 READING QUIZ
PART A KEY SKILLS

1 1 Marketing
  2 2016
  3 Research
  4 They increased sharply.
  5 They were the same.
  6 The percentage of M.B.A. students in the U.S. who received job offers where they had done summer internships increased in all four sectors from 2012 to 2016.

PART B ADDITIONAL SKILLS

2 1 b 2 a 3 c 4 a 5 a

UNIT 6 LANGUAGE QUIZ
PART A KEY VOCABULARY

1 1 boasts 2 alternative 3 persistent 4 qualified
  5 survey 6 ambiguity 7 disputing 8 potential

2 1 chronic 2 expertise 3 assertive 4 illustration
  5 diminish 6 extend 7 founder 8 prospective

PART B LANGUAGE DEVELOPMENT

3 1 information technology 2 training program
  3 household income 4 work-life balance
  5 job market

UNIT 6 WRITING QUIZ
PART A GRAMMAR FOR WRITING

1 1 are shown   2 supports   3 is demonstrated
   4 indicates   5 suggests

PART B WRITING TASK

2 *Answers will vary.*

UNIT 7 READING QUIZ
PART A KEY SKILLS

1 1 a   2 c   3 c   4 b   5 b

PART B ADDITIONAL SKILLS

2 1 T
   2 T
   3 DNS
   4 F; Brazil was *among* the countries hit hard, meaning
      it was not the only one.
   5 DNS
   6 DNS
   7 F; Although Zika can be controlled and cases are
      diminishing, it may not be possible to eradicate
      the virus completely, meaning it probably
      won't disappear.

UNIT 7 LANGUAGE QUIZ
PART A KEY VOCABULARY

1 1 cycle   2 eradicated   3 bounced back   4 grim
   5 proximity   6 mild   7 surge   8 transmission

2 1 countered   2 domesticated   3 confined
   4 therapeutic   5 revolutionized   6 detection
   7 facilitate   8 thrive

PART B LANGUAGE DEVELOPMENT

3 1 affect   2 promote   3 triggered   4 is a factor in
   5 permits

4 1 prevent   2 transmission   3 therapy   4 infected
   5 resistant

UNIT 7 WRITING QUIZ
PART A GRAMMAR FOR WRITING

1 1 results in   2 Because   3 As a consequence
   4 so that   5 due to

PART B WRITING TASK

2 *Answers will vary.*

UNIT 8 READING QUIZ
PART A KEY SKILLS

1 1 a   2 c   3 b   4 a   5 a

PART B ADDITIONAL SKILLS

2 *Answers will vary. Possible answers.*
   1 writers / project managers / corporate consultants /
      doctors / nurses / graphic designers
   2 ability to choose when and where you want to
      work / ability to decline jobs you don't like / chance
      to collaborate with different people and companies
   3 no predictable salary / have to do unwanted
      administrative tasks / must constantly look for
      work / may have to take on too much work to pay
      bills / have to manage themselves
   4 people who are thinking about becoming
      freelancers
   5 It is important for anyone thinking about becoming
      a freelancer to consider the pros and cons.

UNIT 8 LANGUAGE QUIZ
PART A KEY VOCABULARY

1 1 accomplished   2 distraction   3 apparently
   4 detract from   5 gesture   6 underlie
   7 coordinate   8 declined

2 1 display   2 consistent   3 isolate   4 enhance
   5 differentiate   6 phenomenon   7 exclusively
   8 fundamental

PART B LANGUAGE DEVELOPMENT

3 *Answers will vary. Possible answers:*
   1 it is widely believed
   2 loved by many/most people
   3 Italians typically/generally eat
   4 you are likely to/will probably love it
   5 Italy is a relatively rich country

UNIT 8 WRITING QUIZ
PART A GRAMMAR FOR WRITING

1 *Answers will vary. Possible answers:*

1 <u>Many people think</u> that the legal drinking age in the U.S. should be lowered to 18, when people are allowed to vote and serve in the military. *Nevertheless, the law requiring people to be 21 to consume alcohol saves thousands of lives every year.*

2 Testing of medication on animals <u>may provide</u> important health information. *However, animal testing is not ethical, and it can hurt or kill animals, which is not right.*

3 <u>It is true that</u> the government takes a lot of tax money out of its citizens' paychecks. *While it is true that the government takes a lot of tax money out of its citizens' paychecks, we must remember that the government provides important services that we all need, such as policing and road maintenance.*

4 Some children <u>may be</u> motivated to get better grades if their parents give them money as a reward. *Despite the fact that some children may be motivated to get better grades if their parent give them money as a reward, it is better if they try to get good grades through their own motivation to succeed.*

5 <u>There is no doubt</u> that some students feel homesick when they study abroad. *In the end, however, the valuable experience such an opportunity provides will be worth it.*

PART B WRITING TASK

2 *Answers will vary.*

CREDITS

The authors and publishers acknowledge the following sources of copyright material and are grateful for the permissions granted. While every effort has been made, it has not always been possible to identify the sources of all the material used, or to trace all copyright holders. If any omissions are brought to our notice, we will be happy to include the appropriate acknowledgements on reprinting and in the next update to the digital edition, as applicable.

Front cover photographs by (man) Dean Drobot/Shutterstock and (background) vichie81/Shutterstock.

Corpus
Development of this publication has made use of the Cambridge English Corpus (CEC). The CEC is a multi-billion word computer database of contemporary spoken and written English. It includes British English, American English, and other varieties of English. It also includes the Cambridge Learner Corpus, developed in collaboration with the University of Cambridge ESOL Examinations. Cambridge University Press has built up the CEC to provide evidence about language use that helps to produce better language teaching materials

Cambridge Dictionaries
Cambridge dictionaries are the world's most widely used dictionaries for learners of English. The dictionaries are available in print and online at dictionary.cambridge.org. Copyright © Cambridge University Press, reproduced with permission.

Typeset by emc design ltd

NOTES

NOTES